A Year of Encouragement

Charles B. Graham

A Year of Encouragement
by Charles B. Graham

Printed in the United States of America

ISBN 1-594678-48-0

www.xulonpress.com

Look what others are saying about
A Note of Encouragement…

What a great way to start my day—with a chuckle and time spent with the Lord!

What a timely message! How I needed to hear this message today.

I laughed until tears came to my eyes! The Lord definitely has a way of putting us in our place!

This different point of view really made me think.

Your last Note inspired me into sending letters of encouragement to some of the people I know.

We go to a small church and I teach a class of teenagers, ages from 13 to 18. Every week I read them A Note of Encouragement.

It is very uplifting as I look forward to it every week!

Your Notes have really encouraged me and help me start off the week thinking about my relationship with God.

This is going to stick with me this whole week. Thanks for the strength!

If you find this book a source of encouragement, you are invited to subscribe to *A Note of Encouragement* at our website.

<u>www.ciloa.org</u>

A Year of Encouragement

Ciloa

Encouraging one another
us long as it is called Today!

Charles B. Graham
Executive Director

Dedication

*A*lways first and foremost, we dedicate *A Year of Encouragement* to God, our Heavenly Father. He is the true source of all encouragement, the one constant in an ever-changing world. Whatever comfort you may find in the words of this book come from His heart.

We also dedicate this book to our fellow brothers and sisters in Christ…

…to those who at times struggle in this world and don't find the love and encouragement from others that should be theirs,

…to those who see opportunities come to encourage another, but sadly let them pass because they aren't sure what to say or do, and

…to those who still seek to discover if God even exists and look to us hoping to find Him.

We pray that in the following pages you will rediscover joy, laughter, strength, wisdom, and a better understanding of what it means to be a part of the family of God. We hope that as you read these stories and thoughts of what the Christian life really is, you will find truth and frankness that will help you experience a depth of encouragement that we have come to know and that we want to share with you.

May we all encourage one another as long as it is called Today!

Table of Contents

Acknowledgements

A Year of Encouragement represents the combined efforts of many people. When the first **Note of Encouragement** was sent out through the wonderful world of the Internet, we had no idea it would grow to become such a significant source of encouragement for so many Christians around the world. It is with grateful hearts that we deeply thank the following for their work, love, support, and, yes, encouragement.

Our Directors, past and present, for seeing and embracing the vision: Dana Abernathy, Joyce Abernathy, Ray Booher, Susan Furlow, Beverly Graham, Hal Harris, John McMath, Susan Paradise, Linda Smith, Frank Stanley, and Karen Waller; with a special nod to Joyce and Beverly for reviewing material and working diligently in the development of this project, and to Hal and his wonderful wife, Brenda, for researching, sifting through and handling the many issues that arose in the publishing of this book.

The Ciloa Note Advisory Panel, for spending countless hours reviewing past **Notes**, providing invaluable guidance, and encouraging us through the months: Steve Day, Gail Dover, Donna Fambrough, Mary Kay Harman, Karen

Hindson, Judy McCall, and Vicki Parker.

Our special contributors without whom many of the following pages would be blank: Brett Barnes, Beverly Graham, Adrienne Paradise, and Susan Paradise.

Everyone over the years who took the time to reply to the **Notes**, sending us your thoughts, prayers, love and support. You will never know how often your own 'note of encouragement' inspired us, kept this ministry going, and, as a result, how many thousands across the world have benefited because you decided to encourage us.

And a very special note of thanks to John McMath, for expressing a deep passion for *A Year of Encouragement*, renewing that passion in the rest of us when it had begun to fade, getting us organized and on track, and prodding, badgering, harassing, and doing whatever was necessary for me to stay on schedule, which is a miracle in itself.

Chuck Graham
Executive Director

Ciloa...Encouraging one another as long as it is called Today!

Foreword

Why We Do What We Do

*See to it, brothers, that none of you has a sinful,
unbelieving heart that turns away from the living
God. <u>But encourage one another daily, as long as it
is called Today,</u> so that none of you may be
hardened by sin's deceitfulness.* Hebrews 3:12-13

*W*hen **A Note of Encouragement** appeared on
January 1, 2001, I have to admit that I thought this
new effort of ours would be short-lived and reach only a few
people at best. But in just a few weeks I discovered I was
very wrong. None of us had any idea that God would take
these **Notes** to people around the world. And in a year's
time, the **Note** was being read by people in 34 countries on
6 continents. It has truly been an incredible adventure for us
in *Ciloa*.

Among the wonderful blessings we have received are
the many responses to the **Notes of Encouragement**. Some
simply voice their agreement with something that was

mentioned, while others go much deeper, sharing their struggles and what God has done in their lives. It's amazing, really. We never know just how God will use the **Notes**, but we are very thankful He does.

I once received an email that went straight to the heart of this ministry. "Your messages are so delightful every week. Thank you for your ministry and for your faithfulness to encourage us in the Church. Frankly I need encouragement, and you always hit the right note of humor and depth. Why you do this is unclear to me; a call from God, I suppose. But thank you, thank you!"

Why do we do this? Is it a calling from God? Absolutely! But that only tells part of the story. This man's words were very gracious and much appreciated, but truth be told, there's a lot more of God than us in these **Notes**. When they touch the heart, that's God's doing. We try very hard to write what He tells us and say what He wants. He always knows that special someone who needs that special message on that special day. And there lies the reason for the calling. On any given day, there are millions of people who need encouragement. Over time, we will all need it.

The Body of Christ is a diverse bunch of people with different gifts, talents, and skills. If it is to function properly, all of these differences must come together in a coordinated effort. Critical to this effort is encouragement. Through encouragement we are taught, corrected, led, and loved. It is the means through which Christians are unified and the Body is truly built up. Encouragement is the purest expression of Jesus' new command that we love one another.

There is a desperate need for encouragement among <u>all</u> Christians. So many talk a good game, but really do very little. There can be no love where there's no action, and there can be no encouragement where there's no caring. Many are hurt, depressed, lonely, afraid, and confused. This world can be a very harsh place, and sometimes even the

Church falls short. Instead of helping people discover their spiritual gifts, we give them jobs to do. Instead of encouraging them to exercise those gifts as <u>God</u> has directed them, we demand they use them as <u>we</u> see fit.

Far too often acts of encouragement drown in a flood of discouragement. That must stop. We cannot honor Jesus if we are failing to encourage those around us. And we cannot build each other up if we are beating each other down. We must show the world that we are different and the life we have been given is something worth having. We need each other. Even a little effort can brighten another person's day, provide hope, give comfort, or just simply let others know they're not alone.

I love being in the mountains. From way up high, surrounding hills look like a soft, rumpled blanket. Lakes sparkle with the reflection of the sun. Big puffy white clouds stand as the only things between me and the bright blue expanse of sky. The view is always a thrilling sight, even when I get to my destination by car. But it's never as satisfying as when I've hiked the valleys, climbed the steep trails, crossed the gaps, run the ridges, and struggled to the very top, sometimes literally forcing one foot in front of the other until I'm finally there. The view means more somehow. It's not just reaching a goal; it's the realization of where I've been and what I've gone through to get there.

And there's something else. When I'm on top of the mountain, I can see the vastness of creation stretching out before me. The lower hills, ridges, lakes and countryside. But...when I'm in the valley...only then can I truly see the glory and wonder of the mountain itself.

It is my prayer that as you journey through life, may you have the clarity of mind to stop every now and then, understand where you are, look up, see our loving God and be encouraged. And as you continue your journey, remember to encourage those around you. God will provide the opportunity; you must provide the desire.

> *May our Lord Jesus Christ himself and God our Father, who loved us and by his grace gave us eternal encouragement and good hope, encourage your hearts and strengthen you in every good deed and word.*
>
> 2 Thessalonians 2:16-17

Take care and be God's.

Chuck

Introduction

A Note of Encouragement, as our readers over the years have discovered, is a bit...well...different. It has never been our goal to create some great theological work. We'll gladly leave that to others. Instead, we simply wanted to share our own experiences and thoughts about what it means to be a Christian and how we all need each other to make it through what is often a very difficult life. We tell of joy and sorrow, courage and fear, success and failure...and not only for those critical moments but for the routine days as well. After all, there are far more of those.

A Year of Encouragement is a collection of **Notes** we published in 2001 and 2002. They deal with everything from those funny times when we take ourselves too seriously to a time of terror when perhaps we did not take the evil in this world seriously enough. They're about lives, ours and yours, and how we remain in God's love. Most have been written by Chuck Graham, Executive Director of Ciloa, but we also have several other contributors who add their own unique observations. And we've also included some of the many responses our readers have sent us, slightly edited for their privacy. There you'll find different perspectives and even more to think about as they share their own thoughts and experiences.

Keeping true to form, this book is also a bit different. There are 52 **Notes,** one for each week of the year for you to read, think about, and maybe even use in your own life. But unlike most devotionals, you can start *A Year of Encouragement* at any time. January or July. It doesn't matter. And if you miss a week, just pick up where you left off. We want to encourage you, not make you feel guilty for not sticking to someone else's schedule. And for those holidays and special events, we've got you covered. In a section called "Remembering...", we've placed a special **Note** for each of those times.

We have also developed an extensive topic and scripture index that you'll find very useful, both for your own encouragement and as a great aid as you seek to encourage others. Sometimes, regardless of what **Note** may be next in line, the time calls for a special word. With this index you'll be able to find the encouragement you need.

But most of all, we want you to have fun. *A Year of Encouragement* is written by ordinary people who take an extraordinary view of life. We hope and pray that in these pages you will truly find encouragement and discover within yourself a growing desire to be an active part of this thing we call the "family of God"

Notes of Encouragement

When Things Are Not What They Seem

May God bless you this day…even as others are watching!

Things are not always what they seem.

I began my law career more than 25 years ago and I thought I was going to be a great courtroom attorney. Righting the wrongs of this world and coming to the rescue of the little guy. To prepare, I took on as much courtroom work as I could. Once, I had to argue before a court in Metro Atlanta and I threw myself into the preparation of the case. I researched, wrote outlines, double checked the law, and researched some more. Then the morning of the hearing came. The other attorney went first and quickly presented his argument. Finally it was my turn. I stood up, faced the judge, and began to speak so eloquently and intelligently, cleverly laying out the nature of the issues, the clear directions mandated by the law, and the obvious and most reasonable conclusions…that just happened to coincide with what I wanted.

When I closed my argument and returned to my seat, I knew I had the judge in the palm of my hand. He had never taken his eyes off me. Surely he had been mesmerized by my skill, my awesome abilities as a litigator. Then the judge looked at me with a broad smile on his face. "Mr. Graham, I find in favor of your client." "Thank you, your Honor," I replied so humbly. "Oh, no. Thank you," he said as his smile grew even larger. "This has been a most pleasant way for me to start my day."

I thanked the judge again, patted my own back, and walked out of the courtroom. The judge, still with that huge smile on his face, closely watched from behind the bench. "I really must be fantastic," I thought.

Strolling down the corridor, I passed a long mirror

hanging on one wall. I looked directly into it as I walked by, expecting to see the image of a brilliant young attorney striding confidently along. Instead, I saw the rather comical face of a silly looking "rookie" lawyer, a face that still had 4 tiny pieces of toilet paper stuck to it from where it had been nicked during its morning shave.

Alas, things are not always what they seem.

This would be good for us all to remember, especially when we consider how others see us. As you prepare to do battle this day, in whatever form or fashion that may be for you, remember to look clearly. Take the time to understand what's going on. Know as much as you can. Don't make assumptions. Be considerate, gentle, kind and patient in your relations with others...and with yourself. And always remember...

> *...let your light shine before others that they may see your good deeds and praise your Father in heaven...*
> Matthew 5:16

We need to make the effort to see ourselves through the eyes of those around us, for we never know how our actions can affect someone we never even knew was watching.

Take care and be God's.

From our readers...

— I loved it! You are so right. People are often not what they look like or seem either. After my daughter graduated college and was out looking for her career, she wanted to be in the business world until she got there...she is beautiful and carries herself well so she was always chosen for these huge positions in sales, etc...they never knew what the true person inside her was. She grew to hate the business world

because it was not her. People are not always what they seem...

— I loved the story. One lesson that I think from the story is that we should not take ourselves too seriously.

And I will be with you...always

May God bless you this day...with His presence!

I've had a tough couple of weeks. This will give you a feel for the sadness of my life so that you can summon the appropriate level of sympathy. (1) My son's car, recently purchased to replace one that had worn out, broke down. (2) Someone I've been trying to be a Christian example to has decided to ignore God for a while, reject His instructions for how he should live, and not let on to others that he's a Christian. (3) An attorney tried to bring me before a court to testify as to what a client once said to me in confidence. (4) A Christian leader I know boldly praised and supported false teaching after I begged him and others to first seek the truth.

Not a good week on the home front. And as I tend to do, I began my own process of grumbling, criticizing, questioning, and judging...which accomplished nothing but getting me depressed, angry and feeling very much alone. So, after missing a couple of nights' sleep, I decided to do something very novel. I would pray about it. I might not get "the" answer right away, but at least it would give me another opportunity to complain.

"So, Jesus, what do you think about that car? I haven't been a bad person. Why did that happen? We'd just replaced the old car. I don't have that kind of money to throw away. Why do these things always happen to me?"

"When I taught my disciples, those who followed me, and even the few Romans and Pharisees who would listen, I walked everywhere. And everything I wanted done was done."

"Yeah, well, that was then, this is now. But what about this Christian example stuff? I mean, for crying out loud, I've worked hard on that. Sometimes it looks like it's been a royal waste of time."

"Sure, sure. Peter...you remember Peter...he left me in

the lurch once. Even told people he had never known me, and after we'd been together constantly for about three years."

"OK, but we're talking about my problems here. Like what that lawyer did…trying to drag me into court to testify on something I was not about to discuss. He knew what he was doing was wrong!"

"Sounds like that little confrontation I had in the Sanhedrin when they arrested me and tried to make me answer their questions. I was even beaten, and they knew it was wrong, too."

"I'm sorry about that, really I am, but could we get back to me? I'm trying to say what you tell me to say, but others teach something entirely different…people who say they follow you."

"The Pharisees and Sadducees were a part of my problem back then. I spoke the truth, but they taught what they wanted to hear. Everything was a formula, a plan. 'Follow these rules and procedures, then you'll be right with God and have what you want', they'd say. And the people…they followed right after them. They were so caught up in what they wanted their God in heaven to do for them, they had forgotten about simply seeking His will. Success was measured in treasures on earth, not in heaven."

As I prayed, read God's Word, and thought about what Jesus went through, it suddenly dawned on me. And it wasn't one of those stern lessons, like "Get your priorities straight" or "Stop your whining." It was very simply and very gently… *"I am with you always, even to the end of the age."* (Matthew 28:20)

Regardless of the difficulties we have in life, which can be many and of great magnitude, Jesus is with us…every moment of every day. And in those times when we cry out, "I am discouraged, frustrated, sad, angry, and I feel abandoned and alone, as though no one is willing to take the stand with me," Jesus gently says, *"Been there, done that. I know just how you feel."* He understands!

In the trials this week will bring, don't forget…what a friend we have in Jesus!

Take care and be God's.

From our readers…

— Remember that the closer you get to Him, the stronger the battle rages. I always thought this when I would hear how the enemy tried to influence the lives of some friends and all of their trials. Take your strength from Him as these things happen and rejoice in the closeness of His presence. I know…easier said than done!

— You just hit a nerve, this has not been a great week, but it feels good to know there are other fellow believers that are struggling too, at least you don't feel so alone. Together we can serve as encouragement to each other as well as remind ourselves we should look up to our Heavenly Father instead of looking downcast and simply saying, "Woe is me." Thanks for being there.

— Sometimes Christians forget that to share their load with other Christians will make their load lighter.

— Thank you. I guess if we never had any valleys, we could not appreciate the mountain tops. But it sure gets tiring when there are so many valleys. Right?

— As I was opening this e-mail, I got a call from my boss this morning and he told me that in all probability my job would eventually be eliminated. How's that for a start to a Monday? Once upon a time, I would have blown my top or sought revenge. Really! Somehow though, I have a relatively

strange peace about this. Then, I went ahead and read your Note and it was encouraging. It helped to immediately put things in perspective.

The Gift from Trials

May God bless you this day...with a gift!

*Consider it pure joy, my brothers, whenever you
face trials of many kinds, because you know that the
testing of your faith develops perseverance.
Perseverance must finish its work so that you may
be mature and complete, not lacking anything.*
James 1:2-4

I have a confession. For many years I pretty much ignored these verses. They just didn't make a lot of sense to me. "Consider it pure joy whenever I face trials of many kinds?" James must have been a loon. But surely not. Maybe he simply misunderstood God. After all, people get sick, unemployed, and mistreated. Many are innocent victims of crime and natural disasters. They lose their homes, savings, spouses, children, parents and friends. James just had to be wrong. But he wasn't.

This passage looks to facing a trial as part of a spiritual growth process. James is not saying we should or will be "happy", but that we are to see the experience as one for joy. Whether the trial is on the horizon and we are considering our attitude as it approaches...whether we are in the midst of it and are simply trying to survive...whether the trial has passed and we are surveying the damage it has caused...our focus should be on joy. But how can there ever be joy in the face of trial and tragedy?

James says that as we go through trials, our faith is being tested and through that testing we become better able to endure the trials that are yet to come. Contrary to what some televangelists and authors would have us believe, Jesus never promised us an easy life. In fact, he warned us that just the opposite would be true. In this world, we will have trouble! (John 16:33) So, where does joy come in?

One of the trials I've had to endure concerns my hearing. I have tinnitus (ringing in my ears) and a certain degree of hearing loss, which combine to cause me all kinds of problems whenever there is a particular level of background noise. People can be speaking right in front of my face, but under the right conditions I can't pick up on the words. So I frequently ask them to repeat what they've just said and my frustration grows even more as I often hear, "Oh, never mind."

Once I was at a party and having a very difficult time hearing. The room was filled with happy, talking people, and though they weren't really loud, everything was nothing more than noise to me. Then I heard my name called out and noticed my wife on the other side of the room trying to tell me something. The look on my face must have shown I had no idea of what she was saying because all of a sudden the lady next to her focused her attention directly on me. She then repeated what my wife had said, but a little louder, a little slower, and with a bit more emphasis, all without drawing attention to herself or embarrassing me. I not only heard but <u>understood</u> every word.

This lady, though blessed with successful surgery in the last few years, has had a very serious hearing impairment throughout her life, far worse than anything I've experienced. With little hearing, she faced many trials and her faith was tested, but she endured. Did she consider it "pure joy" when she couldn't hear her baby cry or her children speak? No. But by facing those trials, she became more mature and complete...better prepared to carry out Jesus' command to love others...and more sensitive to those who have trials similar to the ones she has endured. She can better understand and help, because she's been there.

That's the real point of this passage. As we face and endure trials of many kinds, we become more mature and complete in following Jesus and loving those around us. Our joy is in the realization that we are now, or will be, better able to help others and encourage them through life's inevitable troubles.

Throughout the year times of celebration come and go, and many remember the special gifts they receive. But there's another gift we should all remember: The gift we can give someone facing hard times...that comes from our maturity and completeness in Christ...that is sincere, loving and effective because we've been there, too. Remember the experiences you endured yesterday, consider it joy as you face trials today, and just think of the gifts you'll share tomorrow. Thanks, Melinda, for sharing your gift with me.

Take care and be God's.

From our readers...

— Unfortunately (unfortunately, that is, from a purely human perspective) wisdom is usually born out of pain, frequently our own pain. But so is bitterness, so we get to choose which one.

Stop, Look and Listen

May God bless you this day...as you stop, look and listen!

"Someone I know is really down and I want to encourage him, but I don't know how. What should I do?"

I've been asked that many times, by newborn Christians and wise devoted elders alike. It's a good question because it indicates that many people care about helping others. They want to carry out Jesus' command that we love each other. But it's also sad because it shows that we are not teaching how to love others. Too often we are so involved in the process of introducing people to Jesus that we forget about those already within the Body of Christ. We assume their salvation experience will leave them not only "new people" created in God's love, but also fully aware of how to express that love to others. That is almost never true!

Becoming an encourager is a lifelong deal. Just when we think we've got everything down, something unexpected occurs. A new experience comes along and once again we don't know what to do. So we learn again. We never know it all, not even me...though I'm sure that's a shock to most of you. As the world changes, so do the circumstances in which we find ourselves. And with those circumstances come new situations which offer completely different opportunities for us to "love one another".

But there is a beginning point, the "basics" to get us started. And it's amazing how simple it all really is.

The Bible describes those who have no relationship with God as having calloused or hardened hearts. They go about their lives ignoring their responsibilities toward Him. Specifically, Jesus referred to them as people who have eyes but do not see, and ears but do not hear. (Matthew 13:13-15) This reference can be found as far back as Isaiah (Isaiah 6:9-10) and repeated later by Paul (Romans 11:8). But like so many other things Jesus said, this has a broader meaning than what appears on the surface. Having a right relationship with God is only possible when we have a right relationship with each other. This simple reference applies to our responsibilities there as well. It gives us the very basics...our beginning point...for learning how to become encouragers.

Be someone who has eyes and can also see. Translation: "Open up your eyes and take a look around." Have you ever driven somewhere and not remembered making every turn or stop? Did you notice the people along the way? When you're at work, with your friends, or even sitting in church, do you ever notice fear, worry, weariness, anxiety, anger, or sorrow in the face of the person next to you? Make it a point to look around. "Seeing" means understanding, and that will come with more practice. But first you've got to make the effort to just look at what's happening in the lives of those around you.

Be someone who has ears and can also hear. Translation: "Shut up and listen." Encouraging is not the same thing as counseling. Sometimes people need a "word of encouragement", something to help them find or keep on the right path. But everyone always needs someone who will simply take the time to listen. It has been my experience that unless someone asks for my counsel, he is not nearly so interested in what I have to say as in my being there to listen to him. Have you ever tried to tell someone how bad you feel only to hear that person's entire medical history? Or while trying to share a personal concern, you suddenly get advice on how to "fix" your problem...even before you've finished saying what it is? Be quiet and listen carefully. Offer advice only when you've been given permission.

(1) Open up your eyes and take a look around.

(2) Shut up and listen.

You want to help people, encourage them through their

difficulties, and be there for them? Start simple…but simply start. Don't find yourself with Jesus asking you, *"Do you have eyes but fail to see, and ears but fail to hear?"*

Take care and be God's.

From our readers…

— *This is a great encouragement! Learning to be quiet and be a "good listener" is quite an art and discipline! Sometimes, just a smile or a nod, or just being in the presence of someone hurting, is all the encouragement needed.*

— *As you pointed out, just paying attention to what's going on around you is so important. It seems like it ought to be easy enough to pay attention, but it's not. I'm frequently reminded of the seeds sown among thorns in the parable of the sower and how often I allow the worries and care of this life to interfere with what I should be doing – like paying attention to others.*

The Champagne Fountain

May God bless you this day...in spite of your plans.

Many are the plans in a man's heart, but it is the LORD's purpose that prevails. Proverbs 19:21

Ciloa is all about encouragement...encouragement by and for those who follow Jesus Christ as Lord and Savior, but also for others as well. This is one way we can show there really is something different about us. We don't just talk about caring, we <u>do</u> it! We don't just support efforts of love, we <u>are</u> efforts of love! We don't just claim to be a Christian, we <u>live</u> it. We strive to demonstrate the love of God in everything we do, and that can be very difficult. Which is why we desperately need more and more encouragers in our lives...especially when things don't go as we planned.

Beverly and I were married on March 18, 1978 (for those of you wishing to send cards in the future). She was my high school sweetheart, the only girl I ever dated. When we married on that fateful afternoon, we had been "going together" in one form or fashion for about 7 years. (Yes, I know that's a long time – although with grown children, that certainly doesn't seem long at all to me now.) The wedding day was carefully planned and everything went right on schedule. After the reception, Beverly and I rode off into the sunset to our hotel in Atlanta, our first night as husband and wife. It was there that my bride began to wonder if she had made a terrible mistake.

You see, I had apparently watched way too many movies that showed all these suave and debonair guys looking soooo classy, and I decided I would sorta use them as my training aid, particularly in the use of champagne. Now, it's very important here to understand that I could barely spell the word "champagne", much less know anything about it.

But, hey, I had watched these guys in the movies, so "How hard could it be?" I asked myself.

After we checked into the hotel and were in the bridal suite, I (looking very cool I might add) sauntered over to a table where there was a bottle of champagne sitting in a bucket of ice. I snatched it up and swung around to see my bride giving me what I now recognize as that "You don't really know what you're doing, do you?" look, which of course I misinterpreted as, "Oh, you man of mine!" I looked down at the bottle and noticed a wire fishnet kind of thing over the top. Odd, I'd never heard of that before, but apparently, I deduced, I was supposed to simply remove it, pop the top, and pour out that bubbly stuff. "How hard could it be?" I thought confidently. It is at this unfortunate point that my memory goes into slow motion.

As I began to untwist the wire, an explosion occurred, similar (I'm certain) to that of Mt. Vesuvius just before the total destruction of Pompeii. The cork, plastic top or whatever (it was never actually recovered) shot across the room at a speed that would've made an astronaut proud, ricocheted off one wall, then another, and finally, with full force, hit the sliding glass door leading to a balcony no one in his right mind would ever use. The sound was deafening. I was certain the glass door had shattered (it hadn't) and the police would be investigating to see who fired the gun (they didn't). But just then, the absolute worst thing happened.

I still remember looking down into the bottle and seeing the champagne erupting. Instinctively, without any thought whatsoever, I did what every boy growing up in the hot summers of Georgia did when his beloved Coca-Cola began to spew out of the bottle. Yeah, I'm afraid so. I quickly stuck the bottle in my mouth. That turned out to be a very poor decision. Immediately my bride, my wonderful wife of at least 3 hours, witnessed her brand new husband standing there looking like some Grecian fountain...eyes bulging, cheeks popping out, with a beautiful display of champagne flowing from each nostril. I almost drowned.

Somehow, someway...Beverly decided to hang in there with me that night. (Of course, that decision was made several hours later when she finally stopped laughing.) And I am very thankful she has continued to stay by my side throughout the years...even when things haven't gone exactly as I planned.

We all need encouragers to stand by us when times are sad, nerve-wracking, difficult, even embarrassing. And we all need to <u>be</u> encouragers. Life is just too difficult to try it alone, and God never intended it to be that way. Look around you this day and this week for opportunities you can seize to be there for someone else. And don't worry about not knowing the perfect thing to say or do. God will guide you. Our task is to love one another, and that's often done by just being there without saying a word. Sometimes, what we need most is someone who will simply hang in there with us...despite our faults and many errors...even when our "best laid plans" go a bit wrong.

Take care and be God's.

From our readers...

— *What a precious story. I have been encouraged. After 29 years of marriage I am aware of the value of a great sense of humor and the ability to laugh at yourself. Thanks for your sharing.*

— *I just had to write and tell you how much I enjoyed this last Note. I mean they're all good, but this one with the champagne was so funny, and I really needed a good laugh and some encouragement today! My husband has been out of work since the middle of February, so that along with a situation with our oldest son had really gotten me down. It was really good to have some humor in the day and laugh along with other Christians. It really made my day. Thanks!*

Newly the Cat and Broken People

May God bless you this day...and all the other broken people.

New Year's Day, 1995. Friends and family had left for home, and things were winding down. I relaxed in my over-stuffed chair, sipped my coffee, and watched as the last two football teams beat each other's brains out. It was then that I heard something at our sliding glass door, a bump or thud kind of sound. I turned around, peered into the darkness, and there, on our deck, was a cat, or what looked like it used to be a cat. He was a large, gray tabby, but very thin. Then one of my kids noticed him. "A cat!" "Be still," I ordered. "Don't open the door. We don't need another pet." "But, Dad..." "No buts. Leave him alone." I turned back to the TV. I didn't want to get involved with that cat. I stared at the football game...feeling the cat staring at me. Every now and then, I turned around. The cat was still there. He made no sound, no movement. He just looked in.

Finally I got out of my chair and stepped toward the door, fully intent on shooing this animal away. Then he looked up and opened his mouth as if to cry. But nothing came. Curious, I got down on the floor, my face just a few inches from the door. He tried to cry again. Nothing. His frail body swayed with every puff of wind. I felt the glass and for the first time realized how cold it was outside. Then, against all logic, I opened the door. The cat moved back. I reached out, but he backed up even more. So I moved away from the door, left it open a bit, and waited. Slowly, the cat edged toward the warmth inside. Fearful but with nowhere else to turn, he carefully stepped into the den...and into our lives.

Over time, we learned more about Newly (named for New Year's Day). He had been severely abused and for a long time seemed to be in constant fear. The saddest thing was the way he tried to cry. He had been beaten so badly and, I believe, cried so often, that he could cry no more. In fact, he made no sound at all. As we nourished him, cared for him, and loved him, Newly gained some weight, became friends with our other pets, and, though fairly old, played at times like a kitten. He had found some happiness. And yes, he eventually meowed from time to time. But he never cried out like most cats, you know, in that demanding "I'm your master" kind of way. He wasn't like that. He was interested only in being with those he loved and who loved him in return. He even seemed to reach out and try to love people who didn't care much for him.

Through Newly, God reminded me of something very important. This thing we call the "Church" is a body of people just like Newly was...broken in many different ways. We tend to forget that, trying to make Church a fun and cheery "place". But it isn't a place at all; it's <u>people</u>, and we sometimes ignore the brokenness that's there. Grief, hurt, and anguish are around us everyday...and we all suffer. Even if we are so blessed not to have experienced such things personally, we experience them through the lives of those we love...but only if we are involved in their lives...if we really care...if we "love one another". As Christians, we cannot escape this. Otherwise, we are no "family" at all.

> *A new command I give you: Love one another. As I have loved you, so you must love one another. By this all men will know that you are my disciples, if you love one another.* John 13:34-35

Every day, people in the cold of loneliness and despair look in on the warmth of love and fellowship we enjoy. They are hurt, some so badly they can't cry anymore. They stand at the door, too weak to knock. Who will take them in, care for them, encourage them? Look around you, what do you see? I've known people with Multiple Sclerosis, Muscular Dystrophy, Lou Gehrig's Disease, and AIDS. I've seen people go through divorce and separation, families torn apart by addictions and crime. I've known people who died in accidents, others who were murdered. I've been with those who lost their jobs, savings, homes, and dreams. They are not simply "all around us". They are us!

Love others and you will be involved in their lives. Are you involved in the life of anyone? When people speak of you, do they mention that you care for others? When you're in a crowd, can they pick you out and say, "You believe in Jesus, don't you?" Or do your actions shout, "I don't know the man!"

In the winter of 2001 Newly died. I cannot account for his life before he knew us, but since New Year's Day, 1995, he got to experience love and caring. I hope we can say the same in regard to the men, women and children we meet every day. Show God's love living in you. Open your door and let them inside.

Take care and be God's.

From our readers...

— You're right. It's much easier to feel sorry for the little kitty than some of our neighbors. My wife and I were talking last night about the lack of caring shown by the church, and the lack of interest in getting involved. I had been praying about this, and basically the Lord was telling me to get involved, be the intercessor He wants me to be, and teach people to fish.

— People who do not understand mental illnesses tend to shut the door on those who suffer with any type of mental illness...We never know when a stray cat is going to show

up on our doorstep. Since God rescued me from the cold and emotional pain, I must try and keep my heart open, because I never know when God is going to send stray cats to my doorstep in hope they will be able to see Jesus through me and know that there is a God who loves them and who rescues the lost and hurt. This I know for a fact because I am the cat in your story.

— Divorce opened my eyes to the degree and level of pain in members of the church. You are right on the money with your statement that we must make it a priority to know what is going on in others' lives. Just one more reason self-pity is so bad – it takes up all your thought time.

When People Hurt You

May God bless you this day...when others try to hurt you!

In all my years of trying to deal with people, I've come to a very basic conclusion...there are a lot of cruds out there. Oh, you know the type. Self-absorbed, ego-driven, materialistic, thinking only of him/herself kind of "gentle creature of God". They can be mean at times and even downright hateful. Sometimes they appear to be friends, right up to when they stab you in the back. And believe me, I know my cruds.

Years ago, I helped a young lawyer get his feet wet in the legal profession. Took him in, showed him the ropes (or at least as much as I knew), and we became good friends. I even counseled him as he struggled through some very difficult times. Then it happened, out of the clear blue and totally unexpected. He betrayed me. In order to better his own position, he threw our "friendship" right out the window, just like a sack of useless trash. Then he spread lies about me to seal the deal. And I was completely blindsided.

But I'm not bitter.

No, really. I'm not. Oh, I used to be. I think at that particular time if a meteorite the size of a Honda had made a small crater just where he had been standing...well, I probably would not have shed too many tears. In fact, I'm fairly certain I would have concluded that God, as an act of eternal goodness, had just rendered His divine judgment. There would be an angelic host singing Hosannas, seraphim and cherubim giving each other high fives. That sort of thing.

And just why am I telling you this? Well, some would say, as they often have to my wife after they've read several *Notes*, "Well, he just tells everything, doesn't he?" And while that may be true, that's not it.

The reason is that I was wrong (I know, hard to believe), and I had to learn some very important lessons. You see, while there may be cruds in the world, that doesn't mean they are worthless and it doesn't mean we can give up on them. After all, as much as I hate to admit this, from time to time, I...yes, even I...am a crud. I may say something I shouldn't say. I may do things I shouldn't do. And every now and then I may not treat people in a manner, shall we say, that Jesus would probably approve. The bottom line is that sometimes we are all cruds (except my wife), and maybe even at times, I'm the worst crud of all.

Jesus said that if we love Him, if we hope to have eternal life with Him, then we must love others. (John 13:34; 14:15) I don't think that means we must "like" everyone. Love and like are two different things. But we do have to love them. And when they do things, such as betray us, sell us out, lead us astray...whether they are our boss or favored employee, next door neighbor or close relative, church member or (dare I say it?) pastor...we must be willing for God to touch our hearts in such a way that we can forgive and move on. Because if we do not forgive others in this life, we will not be forgiven in the next. (Matthew 6:14-15) Jesus said that, not me. If that makes you feel a bit uneasy, take it up with Him.

And I learned something else that will make this more bearable for you (especially when that vision of a Honda crashing through the atmosphere enters your head). When all is said and done, our struggle is not with that person; our battle is not against a human being. The real enemy is an unbelievably evil power.

For our struggle is not against flesh and blood, but against the rulers, against the authorities, against the powers of this dark world and against the spiritual forces of evil in the heavenly realms. Ephesians 6:12

Every bad experience is another opportunity for satan to drive a wedge in our relationship with God, our loving Father. We cannot love if we sit around being bitter, hurtful, scheming, or wishing every moment for that heavenly Honda. We cannot love others...and we cannot love God.

Today as you begin your week, watch for those moments when satan tries to steal your love away from God. And when someone comes up to you and acts like a callous idiot, a thoughtless moron, or even a sinister, conniving, low-life, scum-sucking...well, you get the idea...remember that there really is something else going on here and it's being directed by someone other than the person you're looking at. Take your stand. Love God. And love that person, in spite of him/herself.

And always, always remember...when we put our faith in a person, we will eventually be disappointed, frustrated and perhaps even betrayed. We are all capable of doing the wrong thing. But in our times of darkness, loneliness, sadness, and despair, God is always by our side. He never leaves us. And regardless of what we do, He still loves us to death...and beyond!

Take care and be God's.

From our readers...

— *Your message this morning is just the encouragement I needed. I was dreading today due to things here at work but you put it back into perspective.*

— *Thank you for this one. I said some hurtful things to a friend in Chicago years ago and I think the Lord is speaking to me to make it right with her. Although I did try just before our move....she wasn't ready. So I walked away thinking that was the end of it. But her and her family are on my mind almost daily. I'm thinking to send her a letter of apology and love in Christ. Pray for my forgiveness. I know I hurt her bad.*

The Blessing of Friends

May God bless you this day...with many friends.

*Two are better than one, because they have a good
return for their work: If one falls down, his friend
can help him up. But pity the man who falls and has
no one to help him up!* Ecclesiastes 4:9-10

I am incredibly blessed, and I mean "blessed" in the fullest
sense...truly blessed by God. Why? Well, there are many
reasons, but one in particular is that I have friends. From
Charleston, SC to South Fork, CO, and from Korea to South
Africa. And I'm not talking about acquaintances either.
There are many people with whom I am friendly and who
are friendly toward me. (And who could blame them, really.
After all, I am an incredibly nice guy.) I'm talking about
"real" friends. People who will share their lives with me and
with whom I can share my life. There's a relationship there,
one built on honesty, caring, and commitment. They will
come when there's trouble, pray at a moment's notice, and
stand by my side when others abandon me. They have time
for me. (Some even let me borrow their trucks.)

I've been thinking about this lately because of the many
people I've met who truly have no friends. For whatever
reason, they go it alone, stick to themselves, and live pretty
miserable lives. Oh, they may have money and fancy cars,
live in large houses, and vacation around the world. But they
don't have someone they can count on to be there when
their world falls apart. Some use people as they would a
tool, and discard them when they're no longer needed.
That's incredibly sad. And I even see this at times in our
churches. Too many people keeping their lives locked away
in a safe. No one knows when they've lost a job, when
they're struggling financially, or when their confidence is

gone. They mind their own business. It's all too "personal".

I guess I drive some people a little crazy, but I've always believed that once you come into my family, everything that affects you now affects me. Your business has become my business. I'm not talking about sharing every little secret. But I do believe that if we are a part of the "family" of God, then perhaps we should act like a family is supposed to. We should be able to laugh together, cry together, pray together. We should have a unity among us, a bond built on strong relationships joined together by the love of Christ. We should stand in the gap for each other.

But those relationships require time and effort. True, deep friendships rarely occur on the spur of the moment. And the process can be tough and, at times, emotionally draining as we commit to each other...care for each other...mess up...forgive...and commit again. Sometimes, the love we give isn't returned, and it hurts. But when it does come back, what a treasure it is! I used to wonder how people made it in this world without the love of God in their lives expressed through strong, supportive friendships. My experiences over the years have taught me the answer...they don't.

Ciloa, as an encourager's ministry, is concerned about friendships...the one we should have with God and those among His people. As you go through life, our prayer for you will be...

That people will come across your path who are larger than life itself. Regardless of their physical size, they will have great arms of love that instantly embrace you, huge hearts of compassion they freely give away, kind listening ears that actually hear your joys and heartaches, your successes and failures, and your dreams. They will have warm eyes that see who you really are and not look away. They will have faces that explode with the laughter of a smile whenever they see you coming. And on those lonely days when it seems life just isn't worth the effort...like a beacon on a dark night...they will guide you home.

Take care and be God's.

From our readers...

— *Thanks for this Note. I do have a few good friends that I can count on in any situation. God has blessed me with one really and truly great friend. This friend has stood by me and let me pour out my heart to him and he has come to me when he needed someone to dump on in return. I may not be blessed to have lots of people who I can call my really good friends but I do have a few...*

— *Enjoyed your Note. We have lived in Georgia for 2 years and my wife just recently made her first close Christian girlfriend. It's a relief for me and it made such a difference for her. I have always been pretty introverted, but the friends I have made have always been important to me.*

Don't Mess with the Recipe *by Beverly Graham*

May God bless you this new day…as you stick to His pan…uh, plan!

Have you ever rushed ahead of God instead of just being still so you can hear what He wants you to do? Or maybe in telling someone about an event in the Bible, have you made it even grander than what is already there? Even with good intentions, we tend to add a little here and change a little there. But then it isn't really what God said in the first place…is it?

Take care and be God's.

"Don't Mess with the Recipe"

Many years ago, as a young bride, I had an opportunity to show off my cooking skills. We were having our annual holiday luncheon at work and I volunteered to bring dessert. After days of contemplating, looking through recipes and cookbooks, I decided to make my mother-in-law's famous chocolate pound cake. Never mind that I had never actually baked it before. The recipe looked simple enough and, after all, I had eaten the cake. I knew *why* it was famous.

The night before the luncheon I gathered all the ingredients and began measuring what I needed. Cocoa, sugar, flour, eggs, … But wait … The recipe didn't specify which kind of flour — plain or self-rising. I remembered enough from Home Economics (Family Consumer Science for all of you young folks) to know that if a recipe does not specify then it is assumed to be plain flour. But there was no other ingredient that would make the cake rise. Surely, I reasoned, my mother-in-law just forgot to write "self-rising" in front of *flour*. Measuring the self-rising flour, I complimented myself for recognizing the error and not messing up the cake. After mixing the ingredients and pouring the batter into the bundt pan, I put the cake in the oven and left the kitchen.

Later I returned and opened the oven to peek at my masterpiece. I was horrified! The cake batter was oozing over the sides of the pan and dripping to the bottom of the oven. Not only that, it had ignited and the flames were growing larger by the second. Hearing my startled cries, my dear husband came rushing in. After one look at the fiery oven, Chuck grabbed the fire extinguisher and put out the flames. He looked at me and quipped, "I guess I iced that cake for you!" (I have to admit that I failed to see the humor at the time since the cake was ruined, my oven was a disaster, and the luncheon was the next day.)

Quickly, I searched through my recipes. My dilemma was solved when I found one that did not require my newly frosted oven. Years later when Chuck was developing a seminar on encouragement (today known as **The Encourager's Walk**), he came up with a saying — "assumptions lead to destruction" — and I have always thought he had this "destruction" in mind!

Recently, I remembered this event and wondered how often we Christians are guilty of making the same mistake that I made that night. Don't we sometimes take God's instructions and assume that we can improve on His plan? Don't we rationalize that He really meant something other than what His Word clearly says? Don't we add to His Word to suit our own purposes? Don't we sometimes have the audacity to question the truth of what He has told us?

As for God, his way is perfect; the word of the Lord is flawless, He is a shield for all who take refuge in him. 2 Samuel 22:31

As with following the directions of a recipe, perhaps we

should keep to the simple instructions God has given us, focusing on <u>His</u> plan instead of our own.

From our readers...

— Another example of "not relying on our own under-standing".

— What a wonderful message. I could just see that cake too...LOL. Thank you, Beverly.

Looking to Potential

May God bless you this day…to reach your potential!

Therefore encourage one another and build each other up, just as in fact you are doing. 1 Thessalonians 5:11

"Would you want to be treated that way?" A very simple question, and yet one of the most powerful guides in shaping our witness of God's love to other people.

Whether boss and employee, doctor and patient, vendor and customer, parent and child, husband and wife, or one friend to another…we have many different relationships. Each carries certain potentials and expectations, and how we handle them affects the stability of our relationships. In the Christian context, it can either build upon our witness…or destroy it.

Potentials are those things which have a capacity for growth and development. The Bible says we all have the potential for evil. We can be self-centered, greedy, and never satisfied. But when Jesus enters our lives, we suddenly have a whole new realm of potentials – wonderful new attitudes and desires to learn more about God, draw closer to Him, and share His love with others. But these are "potentials", not "realities"; the good and the bad battle each other throughout our lives.

Expectations are different. They do not come from how we naturally are or can supernaturally become. They are the requirements, obligations and duties placed upon us. They can be reasonable or foolish, Biblically based or created from the desires of this world. But while the potential of good is what we want to develop, expectations are the tools which can either build us up or tear us down. They can easily be misused, becoming the measures by which Christians judge other Christians. And that is not a good thing.

Who are you to judge someone else's servant? To his own master he stands or falls. And he will stand, for the Lord is able to make him stand. Romans 14:4

Several years ago I counseled a church going through a very difficult time. The problem came from a strained relationship between the pastor and deacons. After talking with those involved, I discovered that over time the pastor had made ever-increasing demands on the deacons. He required them to teach Bible studies, be present in all services as well as all other activities and functions of the church, weekly visit the sick, counsel the grieving, evangelize the lost in the community, participate in all retreats, attend every training seminar, and be members of the pastor's pet programs and projects. These were in addition to being spiritual leaders in their homes, servants to the congregation, and examples for the community.

When I spoke to the pastor, he told me of his vision for the deacons and the great potential they had. But the problem was that this was his vision and the potential he saw was one he had created. This man of God with good intentions did not really know the deacons. He didn't understand what they did in their jobs — the time requirements, pressures, deadlines, and fear of being laid off or losing business. He knew only a little more about their homes — financial concerns, issues with children, and problems with aging parents. And he had virtually no knowledge of them as individuals — their health, talents, experience, and gifts. His Great Plan had become the priority instead of caring for the individuals he was supposed to love. The result was growing frustration, anger and distrust. When I laid this before him, he broke down and cried.

When you think of your boss, an employee, your spouse, or a friend, do you look for their potential? Not what you wish they had, but their true potential. This is very important because we are all cailed to be encouragers. But how can we truly encourage someone if we don't know them? How do we build them up if we don't see from where they are starting? How can we have the right kind of expectations, if we don't know what's going on in their lives?

Paul and Barnabas once argued about whether to take a young man on a missionary journey and, because of their disagreement, parted company. (Acts 15:36-40) Paul, looking only at the man's failure, rejected him because he did not fit in Paul's Great Plan. But Barnabas saw his real potential and encouraged him, paving the way for Mark to write the preachings of Peter which became the first gospel of Jesus Christ.

Be careful about requirements you place on others. Instead of issuing demands to make those around you meet your expectations, encourage them so they may be better able to reach their potential for God.

Take care and be God's.

From our readers...

— *I got your Note and it is sooo true. It is so easy to look at others through our own expectations and not truly see the person standing there, only see what we want to see.*

— *I have been reading the Notes for months now and never really quite understood what the purpose of **Ciloa** was...until I read today's message. I am a teacher and am teaching a class of 120 middle schoolers, many of whom have family problems that no child should have to be exposed to. Some have drug problems. Some have anger management issues. All of them have one thing in common, they need someone to listen to them and reassure them that they are worthwhile individuals with great potential. I went* *into teaching to fulfill that role, because I felt called by God to do that.*

In the daily demands, parent conferences, teaching difficult students, grading endless amounts of papers...I really had lost sight of that original calling and become disgruntled. I began placing demands on my students to get their work done and complete projects against a deadline, placing demands on my family to help more with household chores. In the process, I took on a "mean" self that I really don't like. After reading this message, I remembered my original call to this field and feel convicted to put my demands aside and encourage my students and family to reach their potential – as children of God. I, too, am going to focus my eyes once again on God and not me.

Thanks for your messages. I now understand what a blessing this ministry is to the lives of others.

The Spirit of Unity

May God bless you this day...with unity!

On February 8, 2002, the 19th Winter Olympics opened in Salt Lake City, Utah. It was beautiful...rich in culture, filled with symbolism, and at times deeply moving. At the end of the opening ceremonies, the Olympic torch was carried into the stadium. One couple handed off to another – all former Olympic champions. The excitement and speculation mounted with each passing of the torch. Who would be the last to receive it? Who would light the great cauldron, the Olympic Flame that proclaims to the world the Games have begun?

As the last couple drew closer to the stage, a figure emerged from the shadows. He didn't look like an athlete...no finely chiseled muscles, no great physique, no youthful face. In fact, he looked middle-aged and carried a bit of weight underneath his over-sized hockey jersey. Then the light shone down and everyone instantly knew. This was Mike Eruzione. Captain of that amazing U.S. Olympic hockey team. The team of kids who shocked the world by beating the hockey machines of the USSR and Finland.

Immediately my mind went back to Lake Placid and that ice rink. I could suddenly hear Al Michaels once again shouting, "Do you believe in miracles?" I saw Jim Craig, the valiant goalie, skating the rink in a daze after winning the gold medal, draped in a beautiful American flag. And I remembered how Eruzione stood on the podium and then called his teammates to join him...for they were a team.

Meanwhile, back in Utah, Eruzione took the torch to the delight and screams of millions of Americans around the country. He started to walk over to light the cauldron, and then paused. With a huge smile on his face, he motioned once again, just like 1980. Suddenly he was joined by his old teammates...now all 22 years older, many with gray hair, some with none. Then they joined together, just as they did when they accepted the gold medal, leaned forward, and as one...lit the Olympic Flame.

Unity. That's what most impressed me...then and now. They weren't individuals. They were a team. Wouldn't it be great if Christians could capture that same spirit of unity? The world watched these hockey players, was amazed by their past accomplishments and still awed by their continuing unity, even 22 years later. What if the world could see the Church in the same light? What if we didn't cling so much to our differences, but instead embraced what we hold together? What if we stopped comparing churches, and began encouraging and building up each other? Would the rest of the world notice? Is it possible they would see a loving family? Would they discover something they wanted to be a part of?

How good and pleasant it is when brothers live together in unity!...For there the LORD bestows his blessing, even life forevermore. Psalms 133:1, 3b

My prayer is not for them alone. I pray also for those who will believe in me through their message, that all of them may be one...I in them and you in me. May they be brought to complete unity to let the world know that you sent me and have loved them even as you have loved me. John 17:20-21a, 23

May the God who gives endurance and encouragement give you a spirit of unity among yourselves as you follow Christ Jesus, so that with one heart and mouth you may glorify the God and Father of our Lord Jesus Christ. Romans 15:5-6

But how can we ever do this? I mean, it's just a lot of wishful thinking, right? Isn't it important for every church to reinvent the wheel? Can we really focus on edification of all Christians instead of competition among them? Or perhaps, just as with that hockey team, it really comes down to a personal desire to be disciplined, to understand the importance of the "team", to work together toward a goal, and to follow the instructions of the coach. Perhaps, just perhaps, it's more important what the rest of the world will witness than what we individually gain. Do you believe in miracles?

Take care and be God's.

From our readers...

— On July 12, 1996, I carried the Olympic Torch near Warm Springs Georgia. Never in my life have I been a part of such a unifying endeavor! Every torchbearer, motorcycle escort, Coca-Cola support crew, organizers...you name 'em ...were all focused on two things: (1) keeping the torch burning bright and (2) keeping it on the move, one person to the other. If only the church could get a picture of focusing on keeping the light of Christ lit and on the move one heart at a time.

— I couldn't agree more! I grow weary at watching and listening to brothers and sisters in Christ arguing with each other as well as chastising one another over legalistic differences in their various ways of worship.

What does the world see? I'll tell you what I think it's seeing...a large group of people who label themselves as "Christians" fighting amongst themselves over how each of them think others should live their lives. I believe this is largely what is seen by the world. In this day of cutting edge media technology, a person can't sneeze without it becoming national news if the media so chooses.

It is my prayer that in these (what I believe are) "end times" that brothers and sisters in Christ would unify in such a way that their witness to the world would be "Christ-like", not wallowing in their differences and passing judgment, but reaching out to others in His love...teaching basic Biblical truths and letting the Holy Spirit do His job! Just think how much could be accomplished through unified prayer!

In His Witness

May God bless you this day...in your witness of Him!

By this all men will know that you are my disciples, if... John 13:35

"Witness": one who has seen or heard something; something that serves as evidence; a sign.

Have you ever been "recognized"? That's happened to me a few times over the years. Once at a meeting with another ministry, I introduced myself to the new receptionist. She smiled and said, "Oh, I know who you are. You're that Christian lawyer. I've heard you speak on the radio, about how Christians need to pull together." A few months later a friend asked me to meet with some of his friends. As soon as my name was announced, one exclaimed, "Hey, I know you. You're the guy who writes those Notes. Ray, Al, come here a minute. Here's the guy who writes those weekly encouraging things."

One of the strangest occurred while I was backpacking on the Appalachian Trail. I met up with a Thru-Hiker (one going the entire 2,167 miles) and as we walked together, he talked about his adventure so far. I discovered that we lived only a few hours apart and had often hiked many of the same trails. After I told him my trail name ("Stryder"), he stopped in the middle of the trail and asked, "With a 'y'? Yeah, I know you. You're the one who leaves messages for hikers at the shelters saying to be careful and that you'll pray for them."

All of those times were pretty neat and I have to admit that it was hard trying to stay appropriately humble. But they got me thinking. Any of these people could just as easily have said, "I know you. You're the one who...yelled at that guy for cutting you off in traffic...lost your temper with your son…didn't apologize to your wife when you were wrong." Of course, I've never actually done any of those things, but we're not here to talk about me.

The point is that whether or not we realize it, we are all witnesses. And if we are Christians, we are called to be witnesses of God's love. We have seen things. We have heard things. The real question is, "Will we allow ourselves to be the evidence, a sign for others?" And this is a critical question for all of us who claim to belong to the Body of Christ. It is critical because it sets the priority for us as individuals and as the Church. And that priority is…to love each other. It is not evangelism. Now that I've just upset many pastors, missionaries and denominations, let me explain.

Jesus said that loving each other is the sign that we follow Him. It is the new command, an integral part of the evidence that shows we are different from the rest of the world. Some are called to be evangelists. All are called to love each other. Without that love, evangelism is meaningless. Those churches, associations and denominations who make evangelism their priority, gearing it to be the goal of everything they do, fail to see the love fading and with it the sign that they follow Jesus.

But with that love, we carry God's light in this dark world because we know the only hope it has. There is mutual support, encouragement, help, concern, and compassion, all focused toward spiritual growth and achieving a more intimate relationship with God. And as it was said of John the Baptist, so it should be said of each of us, "There comes one sent from God, a witness testifying about His Son, the true light for all people, so that they might believe." (John 1:6-8)

And evangelism? Is that forgotten? Absolutely not. While only some may be called to be evangelists, all are to be prepared to give an answer to everyone who asks us to give the reason for the hope that we have. (1 Peter 3:15).

When we love each other as Jesus has commanded, evangelism bursts forth from our witness of Him. We share the Good News because people want to know why we do what we do, why we're so different. They will ask because in their hearts <u>they want what we've got</u>!

Today, will you be a witness for God? Will your life be the sign that you follow Jesus? What will people say when they utter, "I know you. You're the one who..."?

Take care and be God's.

From our readers...

— *We are role models whether we want to be or not. I'm reminded of professional athletes who get chastised for being poor role models when they do something stupid. They respond by saying that they didn't choose to be one. But it doesn't matter whether they chose it or not. By virtue of their position, they just are role models – poor ones perhaps, but role models all the same. It is the same with us, we can be good ones or bad ones.*

— *We are the only witness of Jesus some will ever see.*

A New Driveway

May God bless you this day...with a new Driveway!

Sometimes we never really appreciate things until they're gone. Take a Driveway, for example. Yes, you heard right. A Driveway. It recently came to my attention that my Driveway was trying to escape. Large portions, more zealous than the rest, had broken away and were making a run for it...well, a slow slide for it. My front porch, obviously influenced by a popular Christian book series and not wanting to be "left behind", decided to join in and had already made an impressive 4 1/2 inches, although it was straight down. Terribly distraught at the lack of unity in the Body of the Driveway, as well as its lack of devotion to me, I called on experts to rectify the situation. After breaking up the insurrection (literally) and hauling off the offenders, we waited for the Great Cement Truck to bring us a new Driveway...one with a better foundation, more resolve for the task to which it had been called, and definitely better staying power. Then the rain came. Just enough every few days to dampen our spirits and delay the Great Cement Truck, leaving us only to sigh and look forward to another day.

During the TWO WEEKS that followed, I learned a few things about a Driveway. Did you know that when family and friends come to visit, they really need that Driveway? It provides a clear path from the main road to get them to your home. It's the way they have to take if they are ever to reach your front door. Yeah, I knew you could probably figure that out. But did you ever stop to think how important that "path-way" is? Without it, many things change. Of course there's the obvious...there's no path to the house and no way to your door. But there's also no way to you.

During the delightful TWO WEEKS I waited on my

new Driveway (Did I mention it was TWO WEEKS?), I found I was suddenly isolated. Meetings to be held at my house had to be changed. Family and friends, who would ordinarily have stopped by to visit, didn't. In fact, except for those who had to be there, no one came by. Even our mail carrier avoided us whenever possible. We were also cut off from our neighbors, because without our "path-way", it was difficult for us to venture out. I mean, my goodness, the cars had to be parked fifty yards down the street. And since most of my front yard is the Driveway, which now was a huge mud hole, it was just easier to stay inside.

I realize this may sound a little weird, but it got me thinking about our lives as Christians. We've been called to be a people set apart from everyone else on the face of this earth, specifically in that we are to love others. And not that warm fuzzy emotion kind of love, but a love that reaches out and touches lives...one that is compassionate and caring... one that doesn't just sit there but acts...one that gets involved. We are to lead the lives that a lost and dying world needs to see. And Jesus is our Driveway.

I am the way and the truth and the life. No one comes to the Father except through me. John 14:6

He is the Way by which others see Him work and move in our lives.

You are the light of the world...let your light shine before men, that they may see your good deeds and praise your Father in heaven. Matthew 5:14-16

And what is that Way?

And now I will show you the most excellent way...these three remain: faith, hope and love. But

the greatest of these is love. Follow the way of love…
1 Corinthians 12:31b, 13:13-14:1a

When we remove Christ from our lives, we take away His example of love for others. There is no Driveway, no "path-way" for them to come to the truth. When we fail to have His love in our lives, we are the stumbling block in the path. We become isolated from non-Christians <u>and</u> Christians, effectively doing nothing…like a great big mud hole in the front yard.

Think about what you've allowed your life to become. Is there a warm and inviting path that leads to the truth…or is there instead, as Peter calls it, an empty way of life (1 Peter 1:18)? Are you isolated in your own world, cut off from others and lacking the presence of the love of God? Take an honest look and work hard to make the Way in your life an obvious reality, so that, like me, one day you can say,

"As for me and my Driveway, we will serve the Lord!" (Sorry, but you should've seen that coming.)

Take care and be God's.

From our readers…

— God can use anything to teach a lesson!

A New Life

May God bless you this day...with a new Life!

*We were therefore buried with Him through baptism
into death in order that, just as Christ was raised
from the dead through the glory of the Father, we too
may live a new life.* Romans 6:4

When Paul wrote these words, he was talking about the transformation that occurs in the life of a follower of Jesus. We change from people refusing to acknowledge Him as Lord to people devoted to Him...who want to follow Him and live the life He taught us to live. Teachers usually concentrate on this experience of "salvation" and the gift of "eternal life" that it brings. But in reading this passage, I've found something else hidden in the words. A message of present hope that can lead us through difficult times. A message we easily miss.

On January 3, 1990, my dad died. For several years, he had struggled with Lou Gehrig's disease, a condition that makes the body slowly waste away. It doesn't affect the mind, just the body, until finally there's no longer the strength to keep going. When he died, my dad was only 57 and my mother only 54. Very young, and it seems younger every day. On that day, after being married since she was 18, my mother began a different life. Though she had her sons, daughters-in-law, and grandchildren around her, she was alone. But she didn't wallow in self-pity or bitterness. Instead, she looked to God for guidance...and moved on.

The next 10 years brought a lot of activity, change and adventure. Though she could not be a doctor as she once dreamed as a child, she did become a scientist for an international corporation, helping develop new processes and products while even obtaining a patent or two along the way. With my mother-in-law in tow, she learned to travel...taking trips to the Bahamas, Jamaica, Costa Rico, Belize, Panama, Hawaii, Alaska, Canada, Hong Kong, and Bangkok. And she stayed true to worshiping God, remaining active in church and going to many women's conferences. She was able to do this because she was on her own and there was no thought given to ever dating again. Then she met Charlie.

Charlie was from Houston, Texas, and had the God-given ability to carry any conversation single handedly. They met each other in a dance class and he quickly became a whirlwind in her life. Charlie introduced a new word into her vocabulary...spontaneity. (My mother and I are very much alike in this respect. It isn't that we can't be spontaneous, spur-of-the-moment people. We would just prefer to plan for it first.) He brought her caring, concern, love...and he made her happier than she'd been in a very long time. On Friday, August 10, 2001, Charlie and Mother were married, and they began a new life together.

So what does this have to do with Romans 6:4? Well, I noticed that Paul carefully says that we may "live a new life." That "newness" doesn't refer to a one time event. It is continuing. When Charlie and Mother married, they <u>began</u> a new life, and every day that follows is a new day in that life. Likewise, when we became Christians, we began a new life with God and every day is a new day in this new life with Him. Yesterday is over. Sure we can learn from it, but it's done with. God doesn't want the difficulties, tragedies and heartaches of yesterday to tie us down.

In *The Encourager's Walk* seminar, we teach that the "Second Rule of Edification" is to take the reality of the present and look to the possibility of the future. Don't dwell on the past. Today's a new day! "This is the day the Lord has made, for crying out loud; let's rejoice and be glad in it." Psalms 118:24 (CIV - Chuck's Interpersonal Version)

As you prepare for this day and the rest of the week, remember that you are living a new life with God, and today...this every day...is a brand new day with Him in this <u>continuing</u> new life. Enjoy it! Enjoy Him! And look forward to developing your relationship with the Creator of the Universe.

Take care and be God's.

From our readers...

— You sure made a new life sound exciting.

— A good example of why we should not define ourselves by our partners, but by our relationship with God.

A New Faith

May God bless you this day...with renewed faith!

*Now faith is being sure of what we hope for and
certain of what we do not see...And without faith it
is impossible to please God, because anyone who
comes to him must believe that he exists...*
Hebrews 11:1,6

Hebrews 11:1 is often quoted when people ask what "faith" is. They don't necessarily explain the passage, though they do love to quote it. But very few look a little further to verse 6. Look what the writer says there. If we do not have faith, we can't please God. But who are these people without faith? They are those who come to Him and do not believe He exists. But if they do not believe He exists, why would they come to Him?

Trouble, difficulties, disappointments, frustrations, tragedies...these come into everyone's lives. How we handle them is determined by our relationship with God. We go to God with many different requests. In fact, Paul told us to pray in the Spirit on all occasions with all kinds of prayers and requests. (Ephesians 6:18)

So how is it that some go to God and still don't believe He exists? Well, some don't think God will really answer them, so they don't believe in the God Jesus described when He said, *"If you believe, you will receive whatever you ask for in prayer."* (Matthew 21:22) But for most, it's because they don't understand who God really is. We are certainly called to pray about all things, but as James taught, we are to do so with the right motives. We are to seek His will, not ours. The many requests we give God are not to be a wish list of what <u>we</u> want, but of those things which carry out God's will in this world. Wasn't it Jesus who showed us how to begin our prayer? *"Our Father who is in Heaven, holy is your name. May your Kingdom come and Your will be done in this world as it is in heaven."* (*see* Matthew 6:9)

Instead of looking to <u>God's</u> will, we become so caught up in our own personal wants that we lose focus. We act like God is a giant candy machine and all we have to do is put in the right kind of change. We look to what we believe is fair and right, good and true...and we expect God to think like we do. But He doesn't. He's not like that. That "god" does not exist.

Our God hears us when we pray. And in those moments when we don't know what to pray for, His Spirit intercedes for us with groans that words cannot express. (Romans 8:26) When we pray with the right motives, focusing on His will, *"we know that in all things God works for the good of those who love him, who have been called according to his purpose."* (Romans 8:28)

Ah, but what is "good" in our eyes? When Paul told the Ephesians to have faith, he gave several examples of people exercising their faith: Abel, Enoch, Noah, Abraham, Isaac, Jacob, Joseph, Moses' parents, and Moses. Then he made this incredible statement:

> *All these people were still living by faith when they died. They did <u>not</u> receive the things promised; they only saw them and welcomed them from a distance... These were all commended for their faith, yet none of them received what had been promised. God had planned something better for us so that only together with us would they be made perfect.* Hebrews 11:13-16,39-40

This past week many suffered, clergy and laity alike. Some lost their jobs, some lost their lives. Some got bad news about their health, some about their dreams. When prayers were made, many asked for what <u>they</u> wanted. And God's answers brought no comfort or relief.

Everyone goes through this from time to time. All have moments when they hope God will be different and simply do as they ask, without regard for what may ultimately be for their good. They do not look to God as He really exists. And in those moments, the rest of us need to love them.

If you are one of the wounded, tell others who can help you bear the burden and guide you on the path God has provided. Don't worry about your anger or disappointment with God. He already knows, and He's big enough to take it. If you know someone going through a tough time, don't judge where he or she may be. Emotions and grief often lead us to say things we really don't mean. Instead, be an encourager. Listen and comfort. Let Jesus' love flow through you. <u>Be</u> a part of His Family. And keep your focus on faith and the one true God.

Take care and be God's.

From our readers...

— I've been thinking a lot about this subject lately. I try to convince myself that I do not want to impose my wants on God and I always tell God that I am asking for what I want, but that if it isn't what I need, to please not give it to me. Nevertheless, in a sub- or semi-conscious way, I often have worked it out in my mind how God is going to respond to my request and I get frustrated, angry, impatient, or depressed when things don't work out the way I envisioned (which they rarely do, of course). When I realize what I've done, I usually calm down. It looks like I'd only have to learn this once, but I have to learn it over and over. I am encouraged that I at least finally realize what I'm doing, so I guess that's a step in the right direction...

Also, I get disgusted with myself when I realize how weak my faith is sometimes. In a similar fashion to what I said above, I often discover that I have decided what God is capable of before I even ask Him for anything. I find that I rarely ask Him for "big" things...it disgusts me when I realize that I've limited God, but it also humbles me.

— The more we learn and put our faith in God the freer we are.

— My praise goes to God for this message and to you for being willing and open as His instrument – the messenger. This Note is one to be printed, saved and re-read periodically by all of us. Thank you.

A New Perspective

May God bless you this day...with courage to follow Him!

Many times I've seen God move in some amazing ways, doing things only He can do. But one time in particular stands out...one event...one act that puts everything else in perspective.

My daughter, Mallory, started working at a fast food restaurant when she was sixteen. (No that's not the miracle, although if you ever saw her room and thought of her working...well, since she reads these *Notes*, I won't say anything else.) While there, she got to know one of the managers, a nice hard working, 19 year old guy who, though working for a Christian company and surrounded by many Christian employees, made it very clear that he was Jewish. And he rather enjoyed talking about his religion and challenging the beliefs of those around him.

Well, Mallory is not one to back down from a challenge. She may be stubborn and choose not to do something (did I mention her room?), but she doesn't back down. So Mallory jumped into these discussions with both feet, and there were many, many discussions. Often she came home from work, telling me of her conversations, asking about Jewish history and beliefs, and even seeking advice. But she wasn't doing any of this to win an argument. The thought of him going to hell and living a life with no hope greatly disturbed her. She wanted him to know Jesus as the savior he was seeking.

Then suddenly the miracle occurred. God touched him and he accepted Christ into his heart, making Him Lord over his life. I am certain there were shouts of joy in heaven, a huge outburst of happiness and praise...one of the lost sheep had been found. Angels high-fiving each other, ticker-tape falling from the sky, hugs all around...you get the idea. Ah, but now comes the difficult part. He had to tell his parents...he had to somehow let them know he had left their beliefs, traditions, and rules behind...that he was no longer searching for the Messiah...because he had found Him!

When a Jew makes such a decision, it's not like changing from Methodist to Baptist or from Assembly of God to Episcopalian. I have many friends who are Jews and their beliefs are firmly held, going to the core of their being. It makes them who they are, giving them their identity in this world. A few years ago I met a Messianic Jew (a Jew who believes that Jesus is the Messiah), and he told me of how he became a Christian...the extreme joy, the unbelievable freedom, the overwhelming love. Then he described the looks of absolute horror on the faces of his parents when he shared "the good news". They responded, not with joy...but by declaring him dead and banning him from their home. They even held a funeral complete with an empty grave to show their family and friends that he no longer existed in their lives.

Becoming a Christian for many people is a very, very serious matter, requiring deep faith and commitment. I'm afraid that we too often think of our "conversion" as being this eternal happy event, but Jesus once said,

Do not suppose that I have come to bring peace to the earth. I did not come to bring peace, but a sword. For I have come to turn 'a man against his father, a daughter against her mother, a daughter-in-law against her mother-in-law — a man's enemies will be the members of his own household.' Anyone who loves his father or mother more than me is not worthy of me; anyone who loves his son or daughter more than me is not worthy of me; and anyone who does not take his cross and follow me is not worthy of me. Whoever finds his life will lose it, and whoever loses his life for my sake will find it. Matthew 10:34-39

Total commitment, total focus, total devotion…must be on Jesus…to the exclusion of every member of our family and every friend. We must have courage to follow God. I wonder, if I were 19 and faced with the possibility of completely alienating my family, of being banned from ever seeing them again, would I have the courage to follow Jesus or would I disown Him? And yet, isn't this really the same question we must face every day when we're with our family and our friends, when we're with co-workers, employers, employees, customers, clients or patients… when we go into the world?

Are you going to be like everyone else today or are you willing to let others know you are a Christian? Will you act as though you're ashamed of Jesus…or worthy of Him? And while you're thinking about that, pray for those like this 19 year old young man who are trying to take a stand. Take care and be God's.

From our readers…

— *Way to go Mallory!! Goes to show what our young people can do! Amen! Bwana asifiwe!*

— *What a blessing to hear of this young Messianic Jew and to join in praying for him in the coming days. How proud you must be of Mallory!*

— *What a great daughter you have! I know the angels were singing that day. We don't have a clue how some suffer for Jesus. We had a Muslim turned Christian in chapel the other day. What an insight to what is happening in Iraq.*

What is Commitment?

***May God bless you this day...in your commitment
to Him!***

 What is commitment? We are told that the best employees
demonstrate it. True friendship has it. A solid marriage is
based on it. And our relationship with God requires it. But
what is commitment?

Commitment is an assurance or guarantee that we will
or will not do something, and is characterized by certainty,
trust, and freedom from doubt. It is a state of being which
binds us emotionally, intellectually, and/or spiritually to an
ideal or course of action. In the area of relationships, it is
often expressed in terms of loyalty and devotion. The Bible
stresses the importance of commitment in our lives. We are
commanded to be committed in our jobs, our friendships
and our marriages. But why?

Well, what do you think of an employee who shows up
late, turns in poor work, and makes other employees take up
the slack? What about an employer who cuts back salaries,
increases workloads, but demands more effort and time?
And would you want a "friend" who never calls, is never
available to spend time with you, and is only in the relationship to meet his or her needs? What about more personal
relationships...sharing the most intimate dreams, thoughts,
and moments...do you really want to do that with someone
who refuses to make a commitment to you?

The key to commitment is understanding that this
"assurance" is not something for a single moment in time. It
is meant to be continuing — a lasting guarantee. If that is
not our intent, then we can't summon the effort to work at it
every day, which is what commitment requires. No commitment comes easily. It is not a playful or childish thing to
give. If it is to mean anything at all, commitment must have

our regular attention. Otherwise, it's nothing more than words spoken in the wind.

God wants us to take all our commitments seriously. If we cannot keep our commitments, then our words mean nothing and our witness of Him is lost. More importantly, if we can't keep our commitment to those around us, whether they are employers, employees, friends, or spouses, how can we keep our commitment to God? We can't! And we won't!

See to it, brothers, that none of you has a sinful, unbelieving heart that turns away from the living God. But encourage one another daily, as long as it is called Today, so that none of you may be hardened by sin's deceitfulness. We have come to share in Christ if we hold firmly till the end the confidence we had at first. Hebrews 3:12-14

"Holding firmly till the end." That takes commitment. We don't treat our jobs casually and expect to have continuing employment. We don't use people selfishly and think they will be lifelong friends. We don't experiment with intimate relationships and really think it will help us find someone who will be true. And we don't build marriages on "what makes <u>me</u> happy today" and believe we will have anything that can really last.

Commitment. It strengthens us in the good times so we can endure the bad. The same is true in our relationship with God. By being seriously committed to Him, we become better able to withstand the evil and sadness this world will send our way. Being a Christian can be tough, and life itself can be very difficult. Sometimes bad things happen, and sometimes life just stinks.

Have you been strengthened through a commitment to God? Are you prepared to do all things through Christ? Or are your promises just words?

Take care and be God's.

From our readers…

— Dealing with so many who have lost that commitment within the church, I needed this today just to remind me how important it is and that I must keep at it myself.

— I was really convicted by this particular Note. I haven't been faithful to spending the time that I need to on my relationship with God. I have made excuses about not having the time…

Being Who God Wants Us to Be

May God bless you this day...as you be you!

My wife, Beverly, has a dream. Deep in the far reaches of her mind, she hopes and longs for the day when her husband will finally come to that point in time when he is...cultured. Or at least not embarrassing. OK, it's really more of a fantasy than a dream.

Many years ago Beverly set out on a quest: I would become refined or she would kill me trying. And so, trying I became. Once she introduced me to ballet, a world of leaping men and women, none of whom had ever heard of "body fat." And though they were incredibly athletic — even the smallest could have slam dunked a basketball with no problem — my interest soon faded. Then it happened. Two men began spinning at opposite ends of the stage. Faster and faster they twirled, like tops out of control, when suddenly...they collided. The crowd was deathly silent. Well, except for me who, without a thought in my head, laughed. Everyone stared at me as my guffaw echoed across the cavernous room. Everyone except Beverly, who had buried her head in her hands and was slowly muttering, "Who is this imbecile?"

I've never been back to the ballet. Can't even mention it without getting an icy stare. But, hey, I gave it a shot. It just turned out that it wasn't for me. And though Beverly was not really trying to change me into something I'm not, isn't that what we often seek to do with others? We come up with an idea of how something should be and then cram people into that mold. Even the Apostle Paul tried to do that.

Some time later Paul said to Barnabas, "Let us go back and visit the brothers in all the towns where we preached the word of the Lord and see how they are doing." Barnabas wanted to take John, also called Mark, with them, but Paul did not think it wise to take him, because he had deserted them in Pamphylia and had not continued with them in the work. They had such a sharp disagreement that they parted company. Barnabas took Mark and sailed for Cyprus, but Paul chose Silas and left... Acts 15:36-40

Paul was an evangelist with a plan to spread the Gospel to the gentiles. He was experienced and had worked with Barnabas on long journeys. Once John Mark came along, but for whatever reason he left them before the mission was completed. At this point Paul had not forgotten and certainly had not forgiven. John Mark did not fit Paul's mold of what was required. Because John Mark was not what <u>Paul</u> wanted him to be, Paul rejected him and ended his partnership with Barnabas.

It's amazing how God can take something as tragic as this scene and still use it for His glory. Barnabas took John Mark and encouraged him, eventually turning him over to assist Peter in his ministry. Now we never hear of John Mark becoming an evangelist. There are no letters recounting his exploits or tales of great sermons. But there is something very special. It's a book. While Peter was preaching and evangelizing, John Mark was listening...and writing down what he heard from Peter. We know this book as the Gospel of Mark, the first gospel written and the one many believe was used extensively in the writings of Matthew and Luke.

Although it is sometimes very difficult, we have to allow others to become the people <u>God</u> wants them to be, not what we may want them to be. They must learn to use their gifts, talents and skills in the unique way He has laid out for their lives. As Paul eventually came to understand, not all of us are called to be prophets or evangelists, pastors or teachers. And we need to understand this for <u>ourselves</u> as well.

A simple man believes anything, but a prudent man gives thought to his steps. Proverbs 14:15

We shouldn't simply be what others want us to be, regardless of good intentions. We should consider what God wants us to be, and then seek the courage to be that, even in the face of someone else's plan.

Take care and be God's.

From our readers...

— *I appreciate you taking the time and effort to think of, draft, proof, edit and send the Notes each week...Sometimes it's because you or others struggle with life in a similar circumstance as I do or it's something in God's message that I overlook and you take the time to show me. Sometimes...it's just what I needed at that very moment!*

— *I just wanted to thank you for the encouragement the Notes have been to me. As a student summer missionary, it is easy to look at where I am (in the middle of nowhere in North Dakota) and to be discouraged...But God is here in North Dakota and I am His hands and feet for these 9 weeks. The opportunities are limitless, but so are the obstacles!*

...The mission field is no longer across the world, its right down the street.

You Are Important!

May God bless you this day...because you are important!

A few years ago I was at a very difficult time in my life. From my perspective, things were not going very well, or at least not as I had planned. Significant changes were on the horizon for my law practice, my friendships, my family, and my church. Changes which I could not control, affect or even influence. The burdens were very great and I was often frustrated and depressed. I tried to handle everything by absorbing myself in "God's work", especially in the area of counseling others.

Then one day on my way to work, I noticed a church sign that read, "God first - Others second - Me third". That sign made me more depressed than I had ever been in my life. Didn't this describe me? Wasn't this exactly what I was doing? In the midst of my own struggles, hadn't I become even more involved in trying to help others find answers to their problems? Hadn't I made others more significant than myself? I struggled with this for a long time, then it suddenly dawned on me. The sign was wrong.

Jesus once said,

> *'Love the Lord your God with all your heart and with all your soul and with all your mind.' This is the first and greatest commandment. And the second is like it: 'Love your neighbor as yourself.' All the Law and the Prophets hang on these two commandments.*
> Matthew 22:37-40

For every one of us, there is a specific common denominator in these two commandments...me. "I" am to love God and "I" am to love others. "I" am to have and develop a close relationship with my Heavenly Father, and then because of the foundation that is established there, "I" am to be the vehicle through which His love reaches out and touches the lives of others. "I" am loved by God. "I" am important to Him. "I" am not insignificant. And "I" am not third.

Sometimes we allow a guilt trip to be put on us, believing we have to come in last so that we can lift others up. That's not how it works. We are precious in the eyes of God. Of course He wants us to love others, but not at the expense of failing to love ourselves. Remember that God loved us so much that He actually died for us. If *He* loved us, how can we not love ourselves? And if we cannot love ourselves, how can we really love others? I'm not talking about an ego trip here or promoting self-serving interests and desires. But I am saying that there is no second place or third place. We are all in this together and we are all called to care for, encourage, and support one another...to love each other including ourselves.

As you begin this day, say these things to yourself: "I am important to God. I may not understand how, but He loves me. I may not know them, but He has plans for my life. I may not be able alone, but He will make me able. I may not be smart enough, but He will give me wisdom. I may not have succeeded in life, but He will have success through me. I am important to God!"

Make a commitment to say this every morning and watch your world change. It will...in ways you cannot imagine.

Take care and be God's.

From our readers...

— *I used to worry about what would happen if I should die; what would she do, how would the kids cope, "turn out", and even what would become of my projects at work. Over the last several years, I have come to the understanding that God has a plan for my life and the lives I touch. If I serve a purpose in His plan, He will see that I am here to accomplish that purpose. My job is to pray that I adhere to His plan in all that I do and that He provides the means and impetus to see that I do. Looking back, I can see where several events, people, even sermons fit that conception. Many might consider it coincidence, but to me, that is the same logic that would presume that everything and everyone in this universe exists through some random coincidence. I don't know if you saw "Touched By An Angel" Sunday, but they had a very interesting illustration involving a pocket watch. Short form, is it any less likely that a bunch of atoms/elements randomly came together in the form of a watch than in the form of a human? Or is it more likely that, as a watch is evidence of the existence of a watchmaker, we are evidence of God's creation. No one doubts the existence of a watchmaker they never saw, but those same people adamantly deny that they are God's creation. And since we are God's creation, He has created us for a purpose, and that purpose is to seek and do His will. And we, "each and every one" (to quote Tiny Tim), are essential parts of His plan. This realization has helped relieve a lot of my self-imposed stress, although some may say I never had (or showed) any.*

— Feeling ill-equipped and uneducated in so much of the business aspects of a nonprofit corporation...and feeling even less like I was one that the Lord would call to lead anything for Him...given where I was at that point in my life I began to pray for guidance and affirmation that this was indeed what He wanted me to do. He gave me the following quote that day: "God doesn't call the qualified, He qualifies the called". I began to accept that calling...believing He would provide the rest. We're only at the beginning of

*what I know from a human perspective would be a very
frustrating search for funding...however, God has promised
He will not leave us ill-equipped.*

*— I really believe this is something people need to hear and
be reminded that they are someone to God and just as
important as the next person. So often we get caught up in
helping everyone else, we lose sight of ourselves.*

*— I especially enjoyed this message today – it is neigh on
to "Valentine's Day" and because God loves you so much,
you can love yourself. We can never love as He does but
through Him, He will teach us how to have that kind of love
for Him, ourselves and others...Thanks for the message.*

*— This one is especially encouraging and was used to plant
some seeds with an unbeliever by someone I forwarded to
and she passed along. Just wanted to say thank you...*

Savoring the Lord *by Brett Barnes*

May God bless you this day...and may you enjoy being with Him!

Taste and see that the LORD is good; blessed is the man who takes refuge in him. Psalms 34:7-8

Sometimes we get so caught up in the moment that we fail to relax and enjoy the experience. The same can be true about our relationship with God. We may be in such a rush to do something <u>for</u> Him, that we never enjoy simply being <u>with</u> Him.

Take care and be God's.

"Savoring the Lord"

Hello, my name is Brett, and I'm...a lollipop biter.

Okay, there it is out in the open. I've admitted it. I don't suck my lollipops. I've tried...Lord knows I've tried, but I just can't do it. Every time I get my hands on one of those beautiful candy jewels, I quickly rip off the wrapping...oh, the anticipation. Then I pop it in my mouth and there's this sudden rush of flavor...grape, cherry, orange...it doesn't matter. And then it happens. I want to savor it, I want to cherish it, really I do. But just at that moment, without another thought, I bite right into the heart of that lollipop. And just as quickly, the thrill is gone.

For the longest time I had no idea why I acted that way. Why did I rush? Why couldn't I wait just a little longer? I went to LA. No, not Los Angeles...Lollipops Anonymous. Nothing helped. Surely the answer to these questions held the key to ultimate and eternal happiness. (I'm a college student and this is how we act, or overreact.) So, one day I started thinking about all of this. In fact, I thought quite a bit. And this is what I came up with.

I want that sudden burst of flavor.

Okay, so that wasn't so hard to figure out. But I kept right on thinking and I came up with a conundrum (college word for "puzzle"). I definitely get that flavor, each and every time. But then I start looking around and what do I see? Other people still enjoying their lollipops. How do they do that? How can they be so patient?

(Light bulb goes off here.)

Does the way I eat my lollipop describe many people's relationship with God? Maybe even yours? I know that it sure describes my relationship with Him...at least in the early days of my walk with Him. All I really wanted from God was that sudden burst of "flavor". My desire was for that holy rush. I was wandering around waiting for that high...that <u>emotional</u> high.

And as I looked around and observed my "stronger" friends, I kept wondering...how do they do it? Their walk with God wasn't based on some emotional high. They were able to sustain a "spiritual" high by maintaining contact with God. They kept in touch with Him...thought about Him, read about Him, and even talked to Him...<u>every</u> day. They were in it for the long haul. They didn't bite into their lollipop. They SAVORED every minute they got to spend with Him.

Some of my biggest mistakes have come from biting that lollipop. You see, when the flavor ran out and there were no more lollipops around, I filled myself with other candy (sin). I said things I regretted. I did things I regretted. I neglected God...unless, of course, He was coming at me with another lollipop for me to bite into. But God doesn't want us to use Him and then cast Him aside. He wants us to enjoy Him and be with Him forever.

Oh, how I want to savor you, Lord.

From our readers...

— God has blessed me with the opportunity to serve many ministries, churches and wonderfully godly people around the world. And there are often times when my fervor to honor Him causes me to work too hard and too long. The result is that although I may be "doing the Lord's work", I find that I miss being with Him. There is a peace I have when I'm alone with Him that is unlike any other time. I may be in prayer, studying His Word, or simply meditating on the beauty of His creation. But it is awesomely different...and always refreshing.

— How we must learn to savor the Lord and this was a good example of this in our world today with emphasis on instant gratification and quick fixes. We should not dismiss God's urgings when they seem too simple.

— Wow! This Note convicted me of how often I forget to savor Christ. Many times I hurry through prayer and Bible study similar to biting into the lollipop. Thanks for this reminder!

The Search for Truth

May God bless you this day...in your search for Truth!

What is integrity? The Bible says Jesus had integrity because He taught and lived the way of God in accordance with the truth. He wasn't swayed by people, because He paid no attention to who they were. His work was to do the will of God.

The same is true for you. If you claim to live in Christ, you must walk as Jesus did. (1 John 2:6) You are called to be a person of integrity, living your life according to the truth of God...not the ramblings of someone with a title, position, or prestige. In everything, you must search for truth and your guide must be the Word of God.

This is so important today! We live in a time when the truth of God is being tweaked here and nudged there...until it becomes so distorted we can't recognize it. And the tragedy, in fact the shame on us all, is that so few speak out against such acts. Several years ago, Bill Clinton claimed to be quoting Scripture when he said that no eye has seen, no ear has heard, and no mind has conceived what we can accomplish. He replaced God with mankind. Where was the outcry? Yet the real threat does not come from outside the Church, but from within.

Even from your own number, men will arise and distort the truth in order to draw away disciples after them. Acts 20:30

For the time will come when men will not put up with sound doctrine. Instead, to suit their own desires, they will gather around them a great number of teachers to say what their itching ears want to hear. They will turn their ears away from the truth and turn aside to myths. 2 Timothy 4:3-4

In recent years, many church leaders have stepped forward to tell us that faith is a power and if we pray the prayer of faith, we can command God to do things for us. We've been told that living the life of Christ means that we will have financial wealth, fantastic health, and god-like powers. Recently I heard one man proclaim that if we put God first in our lives, we are guaranteed extraordinary business success. Another says the way to have success is to chant a special prayer for thirty days. As Pilate once said, "What is truth?" What are we to do?

Show me your ways, O LORD, teach me your paths;
guide me in your truth and teach me, for you are
God my Savior, and my hope is in you all day long.
Psalms 25:4-5

Look to God, search His Word, test everything! Listen to teachers who can honestly say as Paul did: "*...we do not use deception, nor do we distort the word of God. On the contrary, by setting forth the truth <u>plainly</u>, we commend ourselves to every man's conscience in the sight of God.*" (2 Corinthians 4:2)

And look closely at those who give you a "new" way or "fresh" truth for a "different" life. Jesus said that only He is the way, the truth and the life. Does their "revelation" in <u>any</u> way contradict Jesus' teachings and commands? Have they specifically supported it with the authority of God, or have they spoken on their own? Have they taken the Word of God and added to it?

He who speaks on his own does so to gain honor for
himself. John 7:18

Every word of God is flawless; He is a shield to those who take refuge in Him. Do not add to His words, or He will rebuke you and prove you a liar. Proverbs 30:5-6

Dear friends, be very careful with what you see, hear and read. Even these ***Notes*** are not exempt! Take everything back to the Word of God so that you can confidently say, *"I have chosen the way of truth."* (Psalms 119:30) We must do our best to present ourselves to God as people approved, workers who do not need to be ashamed and who correctly handle the word of truth. (2 Timothy 2:15)

Take care and be God's.

From our readers...

— *It's funny, or should I say, God always has ways of opening the eyes of those who seek Him, and lose their direction. Thanks, I really needed this.*

— *It does get a bit disconcerting hearing all the things you hear amongst believers, and trying to get a grip on "The Truth". Many can put up persuasive arguments for their doctrine. I am thankful my faith is much more than a membership in some grand network marketing scheme. I have prayed to God to show me how to better manage my time so I may serve Him appropriately. I feel like I am getting so busy with life, that He has taken a back seat. I know this is wrong, and I'm not sure what to do to reconcile it.*

— *What good timing God has! I really needed this today. I have struggled with a co-worker here at my office. Things are getting worse not better. I've really struggled the past few weeks about what to do and how to continue dealing with him. I've tried to maintain a "Christian" attitude. I think the problem is that I've been trying to please him not Him! Maybe this will set me on the road to bigger and better!*

— *Great words and so vitally needed today.*

Understanding the Message

May God bless you this day...with understanding of Him!

A while back I made a major purchase...a treadmill. I wanted to get back into shape and thought this was the perfect answer to my problems. When it was delivered, I was surprised to find that the treadmill was in several pieces and I would have to put it together. But never one to back down from a challenge, I got my tools, laid all the parts on the floor, and began to carefully read the manual.

Immediately I saw two major instructions. The first was, "Get someone to help you." However I was in a hurry so I chose to ignore this one. Besides, I'm a relatively smart guy. How hard could it be? Two hours and a strained back later, I managed to get all the pieces together, more or less. A bolt was missing, there were three washers strangely left over, and as my wife will readily confirm, I had more than one screw loose. Nonetheless, I had prevailed. Soon, after my back healed, I was ready to try it out.

The second major instruction was simply, "Read the entire manual before attempting to operate the treadmill." Not wanting to repeat what some might consider a mistake in not following the first instruction, I set myself down and began to read. However, I ran into two problems...the material was confusing and I was in a hurry. So, since I am a relatively smart guy, as you may recall, I decided to put the book down and get on with my first workout. Besides, what could go wrong?

The workout sorta went well. The computerized panel had several programs which looked like they could probably help me, but I didn't know how to work them. There was also some way to measure my calorie burn rate, but I couldn't figure out which button to push. In fact, there were many wonderful things this machine could do. I knew that because I had heard others talk about it. But I didn't understand how to get the most out of my new treadmill. And as for what I thought I understood, it turned out I really didn't. For example, if you want to jog at 3.8 miles per hour, you do not...and I can not emphasize this enough...you do not push the 3 and 8 buttons in succession. After being mercilessly flung from the path of the treadmill at a very high rate of speed, I decided to read the rest of the manual.

Failing to understand God's instructions can also be detrimental. Jesus once told a story about a farmer sowing seeds. A few fell along the path where they were eaten by birds. Many interpret this to mean that the seeds were sown in a bad place, a path where the soil was beaten down and harder than that in the field. It was not able to "receive" the seeds and allow them to grow. In the same way, when we fail to receive the Word of God, His spirit cannot grow in us. While that's true, Jesus had another point that is often missed.

Listen then to what the parable of the sower means: When anyone hears the message about the kingdom and does not understand it, the evil one comes and snatches away what was sown in his heart. This is the seed sown along the path. Matthew 13:18-20

He wasn't saying that no one heard God's message, but that it wasn't understood! How many times do we fall into this trap? We may hear sermons on Sunday morning, attend Bible studies, or listen to Christian speakers. We may read fifty books a year, follow evangelists on TV and radio, or play inspirational tapes and CD's. But do we study the Bible and discuss it with other Christians? Do we take everything we're told and compare it with Scripture to make certain that the message of the sermon, lesson, speech, book, broadcast, tape, or CD is correct? Do we take comfort in understanding man's message while failing to understand God's?

Knowledge of God <u>is</u> understanding (Proverbs 9:10). We can't create it or wish it into existence. It must be sought. And that knowledge comes from studying His Word, God's manual for life. Let Him give you His understanding. Ask for help from godly people. But if you're a relatively smart guy and choose to follow your own "understanding", don't be surprised when you're flung from the path. And trust me. It can hurt.

Take care and be God's.

From our readers…

— I had to laugh out loud at you and that treadmill. I would love to have been a fly on the wall! Nonetheless, your Note was well received. I as well, so many times in my life, have accepted words or instruction at "face value" and subsequently come up short. I shutter to think of the blessings I have missed and/or the utterly important guidance from Him that I forfeited due to (in my case) plain apathy…not being diligent enough to go deeper into His word or to seek out Godly counsel about what I had read or heard. Although it seems to be human nature to always want to take "short-cuts", I believe Christ's death on the cross defeated "human nature" and we have the power (in Christ) to change our habits or tendencies.

— Great! Often we read those books before or instead of reading the manual.

Part One – The Mission

May God bless you this day...in the mission!

If you obey my commands, you will remain in my love, just as I have obeyed my Father's commands and remain in his love. I have told you this so that my joy may be in you and that your joy may be complete. John 15:10-11

I sometimes help Christians and Christian organizations resolve disputes. Such cases have involved spouses, parents, children, pastors, elders, deacons, church members, business people, professors, colleges, and even churches. And usually Christian dispute resolution is something I look forward to, but there was one that was different. For some time I'd been assisting as an advisor in a Christian arbitration matter scheduled for Grand Rapids, Michigan. It wasn't the most complicated or largest case, but I'd seldom had one with such intense emotion, frustration, anger, and deception. Usually I'm a counselor or mediator, but this time I had been asked to testify as an expert witness. And I did not want to go.

Because I've often spoken on reconciliation and conflict resolution, some think I enjoy confrontation. That's not true. Anyone who *enjoys* confrontation is a nut. But I don't run away from it, either. Christ has commanded that we confront each other when there are problems. It's simply a part of loving one another. But in this case there was a lot of animosity, and quite a bit even thrown my way. So I talked to God about it.

"There are some mean people waiting up there. You know what they've done and said. My testimony probably isn't all that important anyway. There are others who can cover the same material...well, most of it. It's just that there's this great sense of dread that's come over me. When I look at those people, I see betrayal and lying. I see people claiming to be Christians, but acting like they don't know who You are. I see so many broken relationships. Why should I get involved in all of that?"

But God never answered. He didn't have to. Long ago He called me to be a part of this, and that's all there was to it. He never said it would be easy, but I have to admit I never thought so much would be directed at me. So I prepared. For more than 40 hours in 7 days, I studied letters, reports, faxes, emails, and charts. I gave up my Thanksgiving holidays to pour over a stack of papers 10 inches high. And I continued to ask God to take this responsibility, one I knew only I could do, away from me.

When the day came to fly to Grand Rapids, I still dreaded the trip. Maybe God would cancel the flight or I would get stuck in traffic or my car would break down on the way to the airport. Maybe the increased airport security would take me into custody for questioning because I looked suspicious. Ah, but alas. Everything went wrong. I had no traffic even traveling through downtown Atlanta. I immediately found a parking place at Hartsfield International Airport, the busiest airport in the world. And I went through two layers of increased, intensive security...in 5 minutes. I had remembered my ticket, my picture ID was in my pocket, and I safely arrived at my gate 3 hours before my flight left. So in light of this obvious intervention by the Creator of the Universe, I did what I often do when His will does not exactly match mine. I sulked.

For 3 long hours I sat in the airport, thinking of the people I would soon be seeing, especially the tragedy of their many broken relationships. I boarded the plane in a rather depressed mood, found my seat, and got "comfy" for the 2 hour flight. Then all of a sudden an odd thing occurred. The man in front of me turned around.

"Hello. My name is Bill. And yours is…," he said, smiling and holding out his hand.

"Uh…Chuck," I remembered, somewhat startled, and shook his hand. "Chuck Graham." I quickly tried to figure out if I was supposed to know him.

"Great to meet you, Chuck. I'd like to introduce you to Lucy, my fiancée." The lady next to him turned around and giggled.

"Hello, Chuck. Maybe I should explain," she said, smiling at Bill. "You are the very first person to whom Bill has introduced me as his fiancée. He just asked me to marry him last night."

"That is so cool!" I said rather loudly, completely forgetting about Grand Rapids and what lay ahead. "That's just great. Well, I am quite honored." I then proceeded to ask if they had set a date, where they would get married, and so forth, until I realized I had probably served my purpose and should just leave them to themselves. So I congratulated them again and settled back into my seat, a much happier fellow.

The trip would continue. Unpleasant people and tense moments awaited me. But I had been obedient to God's will. I had prepared, I was ready, and I was on that plane. And there was not a moment that God did not realize how I felt and how much I dreaded seeing all those broken relationships within His Family. So you know what? He gave me a gift…the joy of seeing the beginning of a <u>new</u> relationship.

God is always with us…every moment of every day. He knows how we feel, and He will comfort us. If we will stay true to Him and just follow His lead, He will take care of us through the difficulties that lie ahead, and He will do amazing things. More later…as this journey continues.

Take care and be God's.

From our readers...

— *I have just finished reading your Note. My initial intent was to use the cutesy "You've been reading my mind again, haven't you" response that I reserve for unusual communications I receive from time to time when others seem to know what is on my mind. Yours came on the rear doorstep of a work-related ongoing ordeal I have been "enjoying—*
—NOT". Your observation has served to remind me of what I already know and have half-heartedly attempted to apply to my situation. Because the LORD has already mollified my current anxiety, your words come as yet another iteration of the message we all have received, but sometimes lose in the rush of daily life... "GOD loves you" and me and everyone else whom He has made in this world He has created for us to live in.

— *I want to thank you...The light bulb came on as I read of these people who were angry, bitter and unforgiving of each other. If we cannot forgive our brothers and sisters in Christ then how can we begin to forgive those who are in the world or how can we expect the Lord to forgive us. Forgiveness has long been a gift from God for me – not only my own but being able to forgive others and move on. As I read this Note I realized I had not forgiven these people. No wonder seeing their sign this week caused such anger in me. Satan has always been a liar...and it's time to forgive and move on.*

— *I truly enjoy your sense of humor. I believe there are no such things as "just" coincidences. Instead, I believe coincidences are episodes of direct intervention by a loving Father.*

Part Two – The Preparation

May God bless you this day...in the preparation!

The journey continues...

The flight to Grand Rapids was uneventful except for brief, though pretty rough, turbulence. It came, of course, just after I got my cup of steaming hot coffee. Trying not to be a bother, I told the flight attendant I would take it black, but she insisted I take two sugars. As she handed me the packages, she said, "Of course, it will go straight to your thighs," and cackled down the aisle. I felt my seatbelt getting tighter.

Our approach into Gerald R. Ford International Airport was pleasant. Night had fallen and I could see hundreds of houses already lit up with their Christmas lights. Even the tower at the airport had Christmas lights all over it. After we landed and the plane arrived at the gate, I stepped out onto the tarmac and breathed in some cold and refreshing Michigan air, a nice change to the stuffiness of the airplane. Once inside the terminal, I called the hotel and 20 minutes later a shuttle whisked me and 3 other passengers to downtown Grand Rapids. On the way I discovered they were from Florida and South Carolina, had all been on my flight, and not a one of them had ever been to Grand Rapids. Upon hearing that, our driver immediately began to give us a brief history of his home, complete with statistical data and a tour of the downtown area (which took about 3 minutes) before dropping us off at the Amway Grand Plaza. We all hopped out of the van, got our luggage, and checked in. Time...7:10 p.m.

Without a lot of detail, let me just say that the room was <u>very</u> <u>niiiice</u>! I had plenty of space to empty my briefcase and spread out my 10 inch thick stack of papers. But as I did, I could feel the dread return. The next day I would testify in a Christian arbitration case against one of the largest Christian businesses in the world. Several people would be there who have been quite open about not liking me, accusing me of terrible and un-Christian behavior, attacking my integrity, and publicly lying about my actions and motives. It's especially difficult when such things come from someone I long ago thought was a friend. But the importance of money and power can certainly change people. There was also my testimony itself…details covering the last 4 years. Would I remember it all? What if I became confused?

In the middle of this growing anxiety, there was a knock at my door and in walked Steve, the attorney for "our" side as well as my friend. Smiling broadly he took a seat in one of the wingback chairs across from the sofa and coffee table where I had spread out my papers. (I told you it was a nice room.) In the short time I had known Steve, I found him to be a strong Christian, serious about his integrity and witness before God. And he was like a breath of fresh air at that moment. For the next hour, we talked about the case and the testimony that had already been given. He also told me of some unexpected issues that had been raised. It was at that specific moment that I <u>remembered</u>…I remembered some critical information that went directly to those issues. When I shared it with Steve, his eyes lit up…and I think we both realized once again just how much God was in control.

After Steve left, I noticed my mood had changed. I felt lighter. And even though the next day would bring confrontation, I had peace…because I knew that regardless of what might come, God would not abandon or betray me. He would remain by my side. I felt so good I did something I've only seen done on TV and in movies…I ordered room service. (Though let me say right here that a Reuben sandwich with sauerkraut and thousand island dressing at 11 o'clock at night is not a good idea.) And my prayer that evening? To remember what I needed to remember, to speak the truth, and to carry out the mission God had given me.

Just before Jesus' arrest and seeing the worry and fear in the hearts of His disciples, He comforted them.

But the Counselor, the Holy Spirit, whom the Father will send in my name, will teach you all things and will remind you of everything I have said to you. Peace I leave with you; my peace I give you. I do not give to you as the world gives. Do not let your hearts be troubled and do not be afraid. John 14:25-27

God calls each of us to a mission and we are to obey, but He understands. No fear, worry, or dread escapes His notice. For our comfort, He gives us His assurance, peace and presence. And we get to be still and watch as He does some amazing things. As this journey continues...

Take care and be God's.

From our readers...

— At ALL cost.....follow God's leading.

Part Three – The Reconciliation

May God bless you this day…with reconciliation!

*If your brother sins against you, go and show him
his fault, just between the two of you. If he listens to
you, you have won your brother over.*
Matthew 18:15

The journey still continues…

OK, so where were we? Oh yeah. I'm at a hotel in Grand Rapids, Michigan. It is now morning; the day finally for my big scene when I would give my testimony. Although I was not needed until 10:30 a.m., I arose very early and began getting ready. I took a quick shower, ironed my shirt in the ironing alcove (I'm telling you it was a very, very nice room), and then looked over my notes for the last time. But there was something missing; something very noticeable. The dread had gone. No anxiety or worry. I was at peace and very focused on the mission at hand. When I realized this new "attitude," I laughed a little. It never ceases to amaze me how God continues to step into my life and take care of me. Ah, if only I would remember more often to get out of His way.

After checking out of the hotel, I walked the two blocks to where the arbitration was even then being held. Entering an office building, I took the elevator to the 10th floor and made my way to a large waiting room, empty except for one solitary figure. On the way I had thought about 3 people I would probably see this day. One had long ago been a friend, or so I had assumed, but now the mere mention of my name made him instantly angry. He was on one side of the dispute. Another was still a friend, but the relationship had suffered under the strain of the dispute. He was on the other side.

The third, like me, was called as a witness. I've known him longer than the others. We've shared ups and downs, good times and bad. I've prayed many times with and for him, and I know he has done the same for me. In many ways our friendship had been close, but it was never as close as it could have been…and that was my fault. For though he had often opened his heart and bared his soul with me, I had not really done the same with him. Why? Because I had convinced myself that if he knew I sometimes had problems, he might discover I'm not the "all wise" counselor with all the right answers. He might never ask for my help or advice again. I so wanted to make certain I could be there for him that I would not open up and let him be there for me.

One sided "friendships" cannot last, and neither did this one. When he eventually moved away, the distance in miles soon became a distance in our relationship. For the past two years, I had not heard his voice or seen his face. Until that one person sitting alone in the large waiting room…looked up. Time…10:30 a.m.

God can move in some awfully strange ways. I had prepared for a confrontation, traveled a great distance, and readied myself for the reality and cost of broken relationships…other people's broken relationships. What I faced instead were some in my own life. The arbitration labored on throughout the day and I was not called until more than 5 hours later. But during that time, my old friend and I talked…and talked…and talked. In the waiting room, over lunch, and back again, we shared what had been going on in our lives for the past 2 years and we described some of our hopes and dreams for the next two. And it was good. I had come to Grand Rapids looking to help others reconcile. What I found was reconciliation for me. I had my friend back.

As for the other two, well, the first forced himself to shake my hand and remained very cold. To this day I do not know what caused the problem, and he will not tell me. I remain ready to reconcile, but the final decision is his. However there is hope for the other relationship. As I left he thanked me for being there and assured me that we would talk. And hopefully we will.

In this time of terrorism, death and destruction, we as followers of Christ have the opportunity to be a very bright light in an incredibly dark world. Jesus' command that we love one another does not end with friends and neighbors with whom we have no problems. We must show that love throughout the Body of Christ. When those who don't know Jesus look at our lives, they need to see people devoted to each other, who take seriously the call for unity, who strive for peace and harmony, and who become so concerned at even the thought of a broken relationship that they will take every opportunity to seek and restore that which was lost. What an incredible witness that would be.

Are you upset with anyone? Do you believe someone has wronged you? Have you mistreated another person? Do something about it. Don't sit back and wait on them, or hide it under a rug and "forget" about it. In God's kingdom, that isn't allowed. Seek reconciliation. Make Jesus proud to call you His friend and follower. And then watch Him do amazing things. Next...the final word.

Take care and be God's.

From our readers...

— *This Note helped me...I've been working on reconciling...Thought I had made real progress then heard from another what his real thoughts are. Very discouraging. One of the worst weeks I've had in a long time. That's when I need to lean on the Father the most...Thanks for sharing what's been going on.*

— *Why are we always surprised when God shows up?!?*

Part Four – The Testimony

May God bless you this day...with a testimony!

Sometimes being a peacemaker can be very difficult, especially when you know and care about those involved. Anger, tension and frustration come together, making many lives quite miserable. Such was the case in Grand Rapids, Michigan. The dispute was very serious, the emotions deeply held, and the effects... Well, in Hebrews, God tells us to see to it *"that no bitter root grows up to cause trouble and defile many."* (Hebrews 12:15b) When someone wrongs another, a seed of conflict is planted. Nurtured with pride, it grows in anger, developing long bitter roots that stretch into self-justification, deception, selfish ambition, envy, and rage. Eventually the roots mass together into a tightly woven ball of hatred, feeding on themselves and preventing anything from reaching the heart of what is left of the seed. Many are affected, and life can become a tortured existence of distrust, fear, and doubt.

Such had happened to some in this case. When the day arrived for my testimony, I could see the bitterness in the glance of their eyes and the expressions on their faces. They appeared weary as from a heavy burden. I felt sorry for them. Disunity, factions, dissensions. No wonder Paul warned us to work hard against such things and never, ever underestimate their ability to destroy us.

Late in the afternoon I was called to the stand and was finally able to give my testimony. I remembered what God wanted me to say and spoke only the truth. For ten months I had waited for this moment, through many meetings, telephone calls, letters, faxes, emails and even 40 more hours of preparation in the last week. And now, after traveling across the country and spending two days away from my office, I gave my testimony, my personal account of the truth. Then the arbitrator looked at the opposing attorney. "Would you like to cross-examine Mr. Graham?" "No," he replied. "I have no questions."

On the flight home, as the plane lifted off the runway and climbed into a starry night, I saw the houses below, their Christmas lights sparkling in the darkness. Then, just before we were wrapped up in the clouds, I saw one set of lights which was different. These lights did not light up a house or yard; they were meant to light up the way. While others may have been prettier or more cleverly arranged, these…in the shape of a simple cross…meant so much more. And suddenly, I understood. I had been given a mission, one with dishonest people, conflict, anger and pride. I had dreaded the task and asked God to take it away from me, but He chose not to. I was the only one who could give my testimony. So I prepared. And the reward for such efforts? For myself, I found reconciliation and the return of a friend. For others, I gave my testimony, speaking the truth regardless of what some may have personally wanted.

As I looked at that cross, I thought of Jesus, God's Son. He had been given a mission, one filled with conflicts where many people would lie about Him, mistreat Him, and even abandon Him. And yet, He came nonetheless into a world where anger, deception and pride ruled. He gave His testimony, shared the truth, and set the stage for true reconciliation. He spent about 30 years preparing and then set out on His mission. He understood our fears and anxieties, and demonstrated that understanding by allowing us to know that He, too, dreaded the ultimate task that was before Him, even asking that it be taken away. But being fully God, He knew that He was the only one who could follow through. And because He so desperately loved us…He did.

For God was pleased to have all his fullness dwell in [his Son], and through him to reconcile to himself all things, whether things on earth or things in heaven, by making peace through his blood, shed on the cross. Colossians 1:19-20

I treasure my relationship with God. So often He chooses to reveal Himself in extraordinary ways by using the ordinary events of my life. And when that happens, God reminds and assures me that He is quite real, He loves me, and regardless of what may come, He will never leave my side. I had a difficult mission in which I shared the truth while looking for some reconciliation. Through this, God gave me more understanding…that two thousand years ago He also had such a mission, enduring far greater difficulties while bringing a way of reconciliation for all who would find it. I had left home saddened by the lack of love among God's people. I returned knowing how much He loves me. In spite of the evil of this world, God chose to come into it so that we could have the opportunity to be with Him for all time. And this incredible gift came in the form of a small, helpless baby born in an obscure and humble place.

May you find renewed meaning in Christmas. May you see God reveal more of Himself each passing day. And may the testimony that is your life be shared with such conviction that others will see God's love in you, know the truth, and one day say, "I have no questions."
Take care and be God's.

From our readers…

— *Cool! Interesting how all of this worked into the Christmas story. I believe that if most of us prayerfully looked at our own lives, God would reveal the Christmas story in parallel to each of us, too. Very inspiring, Chuck!*

— Great how He revealed Himself to you. Isn't it just like God to turn it around so you can see HIM in all circumstances!?

Watch Your Mouth

May God bless you this day...and watch your mouth.

I have this mental picture. There's a dimly lit room; its walls lined with dusty ledgers. In one corner sits a tired angel writing very carefully. He's making entries of things God will "discuss" with a particular human one day, such as each time he says a somewhat careless word. After completing the last entry, the angel places the ledger on a shelf next to many others and then opens a new one. He entitles it, "Chuck's Moments, Volume 2167". With that ever in my mind, I'm trusting that God has a gooooood sense of humor. Otherwise, in the hands of an Omni-serious God, I may be in trouble.

Quite a few years ago, my buddy Jerry and I formed "Friends", a contemporary Christian singing group. We had the privilege of singing at a number of churches, revivals, and conferences over a wonderful 6 year period. Once we were asked to sing at Jerry's home church for a special homecoming celebration. Since he had grown up in this church, these people had known him a very long time. So, in our weekly rehearsals, Jerry kept reminding me how important this was and for me to be on my best behavior. "Not a problem," I confidently assured him.

When the day arrived, Jerry was very nervous. Normally that was my role, but this day I was calm. In our first set, everything was going great until we got to this one song, a duet with me accompanying on guitar. I played my intro and then set up for Jerry's lead, but there was nothing...nothing except Jerry staring blankly into the several hundred faces who had seen him as a small boy. I shifted gears and played the intro again for one more run. This time Jerry sang out, but he was singing <u>my</u> verse. Well, for me this was starting to get funny. After the chorus, I got ready for my part and decided I'd sing Jerry's verse. Unfortunately, he didn't know that and while I sang his verse, he began to repeat mine. It sounded like we were singing in tongues! I started laughing and had to stop playing. But, alas for poor Jerry, that was not the worst part.

You see, it should have been Jerry's turn to talk between songs, which meant my mike would have been dead. So you can imagine the surprise when I laughed, looked at him, and innocently whispered, "Well, that was boogered up." A look of sheer horror crossed Jerry's face as we heard throughout the sanctuary, out into the halls, and beyond through large outdoor speakers to the hundreds eating outside…the clear, echoing words, "boogered up…boogered up…boogered up." Of course, my angel was writing feverishly.

I have since learned that it is not common nor appropriate to use the word "booger" or any derivation thereof in or around the pulpit area. Thankfully, my laughter was contagious and everyone joined in. Well, everyone except Jerry, who had to be given CPR and, I believe, was in therapy for many years.

You know, often these are humorous or, as in my case, humiliating times, but being careless in the words we use is a serious matter. Sometimes they hurt others and harm relationships. *"Reckless words pierce like a sword…"* (Proverbs 12:18) They can divide us and destroy our witness. *"If anyone considers himself religious and yet does not keep a tight rein on his tongue, he deceives himself and his religion is worthless."* (James 1:26) What we say can carry *"the power of life and death"* for others in a very real spiritual sense. (Proverbs 18:21)

As you go about your day, watch what you say. Don't be careless. Someone's view of Christians, as well as of Jesus Himself, could be affected. Our witness of Him is too important. We just can't afford to booger this up. Oh dear, I think I hear someone writing again.

Take care and be God's.

From our readers...

— *As I struggle daily with "boogering up", I could appreciate this week's message more than words can say. Thank you for opening up yourself so that I might remember this week to ask the Lord to place a lock on my lips at those times I might say something that would cause me to be less than Christ-like.*

— *Your encouragement was so good for me this week. I have been dealing with my words especially in the last two weeks and that was timely. I pray I will remember someone writing every time I start to speak harshly...*

A Lesson in Pruning *by Susan Paradise*

May God bless you this day...as He reshapes your life.

I am the true vine, and my Father is the gardener.
He cuts off every branch in me that bears no fruit,
while every branch that does bear fruit he prunes so
that it will be even more fruitful. John 15:1-2

"**B**eing a Christian" does not happen overnight or because we make a single decision. That decision is a beginning point, while being a Christian is a lifetime endeavor. Every day we have the opportunity to learn more and to grow more spiritually. Every day we have the chance to allow God to work on us, changing us into the people He wants us to be. Sometimes this process is fun and exciting. Other times it is difficult and hard. But we keep on because we love God and are committed to being a witness of the love that He has for everyone in this world. We must look to God's work in our lives, as He reshapes us and helps us every day to <u>be</u> a Christian.

Take care and be God's.

"A Lesson in Pruning"

I have a house plant. It's not attractive - rather odd looking, in fact. I don't even know what it's called. At first the only value it held was a sentimental one. (I got it 9 years ago as a "welcome" gift to a new job). Through the years I watched it grow taller and taller. But the taller it grew, the less bushy it became, until eventually it was nothing more than several stems with a few leaves poking out the tops. It was certainly detracting more from the décor than it was adding to it. So one day I decided to take action. Without really knowing if my plan would work, I cut the stems down to about ½ inch from the soil, leaving just poor little stumps in the flower pot. Then I put the stems in a glass of water and placed it near a window. Every few days I checked for progress, but there was no change...just skinny stems and little stumps.

Finally one day I saw something. Tiny white roots had begun to sprout on the stems. I watched carefully over the next few days as the roots grew, stretching out like tiny thin fingers. When they looked sturdy enough, I took them out of the water and replanted them in the pot, all around those pitiful little stumps. I waited anxiously to see if they would survive. Then, a few weeks later, tiny green shoots began to form in some of the "joints" on the stems. I was so thankful I had not destroyed my plant!

But while the stems were showing off new growth, those stumps just sat there. Nothing seemed to be happening. Compared to the stems, they looked ridiculous in that over-sized pot. Maybe I had wasted my time giving them any attention at all.

Then many days later, while admiring my rejuvenated stems, I looked down at the tiny stumps. To my surprise, I noticed even tinier "bumps"...bumps of greenery...and they were coming from each one of the stumps. I couldn't believe it. They had been given up as a lost cause, a hopeless effort...a waste of time. But there they were...alive and well, after all. As more days passed, these little green bumps slowly developed into many shoots, which grew and joined with the new growth from the stems.

It had been exciting and interesting to watch all the new foliage fill what was once empty space. The "old" plant had become committed to growing in only one direction and had stopped spreading out and producing new growth. But because I cared enough to do some pruning and replanting, one plant became many and they were stronger and healthier than that skinny, bunch of stalks I once had. I was pleased.

One day I was admiring how much God cares for plants,

especially that He would design them to grow fuller and richer by simply being pruned. And then it hit me - how much more He must care for us as He lovingly "prunes" us (John 15:2) and how much more it must please Him to watch us "sprout new growth". He doesn't care if we are "unattractive" to others. He sees our potential and knows our value. And He doesn't have to "hope" His pruning will work. He <u>knows</u> it will work! By guiding, teaching, and even disciplining us, and through our obedience to Him, He will remove those things which are not of His will. He will help us grow fuller and richer lives.

And He will shape us into the people we are called to be. All we have to do is trust Him. He knows how long it will take and how much He must prune...even if it's down to a tiny, ridiculous-looking stump.

From our readers...

— I don't know why but I am constantly amazed by God's timing and planning. (You'd think I'd catch on by now!) I used the scripture passage John 15:1-15 in conjunction with Galatians 5:22 for my Sunday School lesson yesterday. A couple of students had footnotes indicating that the words "He takes away" in John 15:2 might be translated to "He lifts up." A landscape architect explained to us that a common solution to poor plant growth is to pull out the branches from within the plant. This gives them an opportunity to get in the sunlight and recover. Then when pruning is done you can ensure that you have, indeed, cut out all the bad branches and prune the weak branches, not mistaking one for the other. (Lots of SS lessons spring from that!)

I then went on to explain the dictionary definition of each of the fruits of the Spirit and compare that to other words using the same Greek root. For instance, we are called to demonstrate kindness as one of the fruits of the Spirits. Another word using the same root as kindness...Christ! Wow! Need I say more about the lesson God taught? Now God has used you to reinforce that lesson! I must confess, as I did to my class, that I have boatloads of work to do. Of the fruits listed in Gal 5:22, it's the middle of the list that I struggle with. (patience, kindness and goodness) I feel the nick of pruning shears even as I type!

— Super Note! I have read similar analogies about pruning, but I like yours the best! I especially like the part about the stumps you almost gave up on... (My 17-year-old "stump" is beginning to show signs of life.) Oh, and the comment about the "old" plant committed [contented] to grow in only one direction. I also applaud the comment about becoming a Christian being a lifelong process. I believe God will encourage, strengthen, and prune many lives through these words. He has mine...

Testing...A Way of Dealing with the Day

May God bless you this day...as you deal with it!

I can do everything through him who gives me strength. Philippians 4:13

In 2002 I had the wonderful experience of having an endoscopy. For those of you who don't know, an endoscopy is a delightful procedure in which a person you hardly know sticks a long tube down your throat, examines the walls of your esophagus and stomach, and then takes little bits here and there as needed for examination under a microscope. Meanwhile you're under conscious sedation, which means a lovely little drug allows you to be awake enough to respond and do what the nice people in the funny looking outfits tell you while at the same time taking away your memory of the entire episode. The only thing I remember is asking the nurse what I should do in case the drug didn't work, hearing her laugh, and then suddenly finding myself in another room thirty minutes later as though I'd fallen through a time warp. I recall absolutely nothing of the procedure, although I've been told I was quite entertaining.

Sometimes we have to do things we'd rather not. This endoscopy was one. A Lower GI series, also lovingly referred to as a barium enema (which I've also had), is another. And for those of you who have never experienced a Lower GI, imagine backing up to a gasoline pump and telling the attendant, "Fill her up." For those of you who have had this procedure and are currently experiencing humiliating flashbacks, you know I speak the truth. But the bottom line (sorry, I couldn't resist) is that such testing is sometimes necessary to determine if there is any cancer or other bad stuff. Though we'd rather not have these humbling procedures, the end result (sorry, it must be the drugs) actually helps us.

Many things in life are like that. We go through difficult periods filled with anxiety, sorrow, anger, grief...times we desperately want to avoid. But we can't. Such things happen. It's the nature of this world to create hardship. And if we will open our eyes, we know this is true. Ah, but what sets us apart is how we deal with hardships. Do we get angry, grieve, hurt, and shout, "This isn't fair"? Do we fall within ourselves and ask why has God abandoned us? Of course, we do. We're human. But what comes next is important.

We have a choice. We can continue being upset about how we've been wronged or this life isn't the paradise we thought it would be. Or we can understand that everything that's happened has occurred in a world the Bible clearly describes, that God is still in control, and that He has prepared a better place for us. And we can lean on His promise that He is always with us as we go through these difficulties, He will give us peace, and we do not need to be afraid.

Trials, tribulations, difficulties and hardships, by whatever name, description or cause, can destroy us or make us stronger. Our weaknesses...self-reliance, pride, self-centeredness, doubt...can grow within us like a cancer, effectively taking away any meaningful life in this world. But if we will allow it, God can use the testing these same circumstances bring to identify and remove such cancer as we focus on Christ and the joy and peace He can give us...even in our weaknesses.

But [Christ] said to me, "My grace is sufficient for you, for my power is made perfect in weakness." Therefore I will boast all the more gladly about my weaknesses, so that Christ's power may rest on me. That is why, for Christ's sake, I delight in weaknesses, in insults, in hardships, in persecutions, in difficulties. For when I am weak, then I am strong.
2 Corinthians 12:9-10

Sometimes testing is rammed down our throats. Sometimes it sneaks up from behind. The circumstances are often not what we want, but what we need. And don't worry about your initial reaction. After you've had a chance to calm down: take a long look at what's going on, admit that you don't like it, and then be willing to allow God to change you through it.

Also remember that these tests aren't just for us. They help those who can learn by observing them. Even those in funny looking outfits.

Take care and be God's.

From our readers...

— *I am so glad that every thing turned out ok in the end. Your Note this week made me remember when my wife first found out she had cancer. She was bitter and mad. After the shock of finding out was over, she had a much different outlook. She, after turning it over to the Lord, could say, "Why not me?"*

— *As the old Skin Bracer commercials used to say... "Thanks! I needed that!" Especially the last paragraph where you tell us not to worry about our initial reaction. My initial reaction is usually not very good. Interestingly, I was just talking to a friend yesterday about this very thing. That sometimes we go through trials for the benefit of others, and we may not understand, or know who these people are.*

— *Thanks again for hitting the nail right on the head. So many times you have spoken directly to me and shown me how to let God be God. Today was one of those days and I really needed it. I won't bore you with the details, but suffice it to say that depending on the person, Satan can even turn a gold mine into a serious temptation and trial. But my favorite of all times are the friends of Job (whose descendants I know personally) that wanted to blame all of Job's afflictions on Job. Those people never learned and are still telling folks that all of their trials and tribulations are a result of some personal sin. May God bless them!*

A Life Worthy of the Lord *by Adrienne Paradise*

May God bless you this day...with His challenge!

Peer pressure and the need to feel accepted are very powerful influences. The following is an edited version of a paper that was submitted in a <u>public</u> high school class. According to counselors, nowhere is there a greater desire for and demand from friends than in school. That means — greater than what many of us experience in the "real world". And yet, even in that wilderness, a voice cries out and a lesson is taught to us...who often consider ourselves so mature and wise.

Take care and be God's.

"A Life Worthy of the Lord"

Challenges...They help us grow in wisdom and understanding. They build perseverance, faith and character, helping make us who we are. And living a life worthy of the Lord brings plenty of challenges. Mine occur every minute of every day. Everywhere I turn, people search for "life", but they are so lost. It's hard to see them looking for happiness in the things of this world that only bring eternal destruction. Alcohol, drugs, sex, power, all sorts of idols made by man. They deceive so many, tricking people into believing they hold the key to true happiness.

The only way to find true joy is through Jesus Christ. People need to see His love in my words and actions, but it can be a struggle. I've found that the world has created a lie...that Christians are actually supposed to be perfect...and all day it seems someone is watching and waiting for me to mess up. They don't understand that Jesus was the only One who lived a perfect life. And sometimes we add to the problem. We are called to live as Jesus did, but it seems that since we know our sins are forgiven, we often continue to live as the rest of the world does. To be caught in the natural flow of the world and its desires is easy to do, and many times we fail to show that God is real because we want the easy way. The result is that many don't believe in God because they can't see His glory living in our lives.

My greatest challenge is to live a life worthy of the Lord and that means making the most of every opportunity to live as Jesus did. *"Let us not become weary in doing good, for at the proper time we will reap a harvest if we do not give up. Therefore, as we have opportunity, let us do good to all people."* (Galatians 6:9-10) God prepares the times for me to share about His love and Jesus gives me the strength to overcome the obstacles in my way. I know this because Jesus endured everything that came His way when He walked on the earth, and His Spirit lives within my heart. Therefore, my life should show how real God is in everything I do. If people can't see God through me, how will they ever believe He is real?

At times the way I live my life means bearing insults and having fewer friends because no one wants to be around a "Jesus Freak." But I remember Jeremiah, *"So the word of the Lord has brought me insult and reproach all day long. But if I say, "I will not mention Him or speak any more in His name," His word is in my heart like a fire, a fire shut up in my bones. I am weary of holding it in; indeed, __I cannot__."* (Jeremiah 20:8-9) When I speak God's Word, I've found some people are attracted to His love while others are repelled. Paul said, *"For we are to God the aroma of Christ among those who are being saved and those who are perishing. To the one we are the smell of death; to the other, the fragrance of life."* (2 Corinthians 2:15-16a) Being the 'fragrance of life' to all who hear the message of God is amazing, but there are still those who are not willing to let God into their lives. To them I'm like a bad smell they want to get away from.

Walking through the halls of my high school, I see so many who have no life in their faces and it breaks my heart. And though they mock my beliefs and tear me down for their own enjoyment, I still feel the longing in their hearts to have the inexpressible joy I have through Jesus Christ. They just aren't willing to risk everything for it and don't want to admit God really cares for them and wants them as His children. They make my life a challenge because I must stand strong and remain patient. Yet my heart leads me to show them God's love and I rejoice in my challenges for I know God is with me through it all. *"If you are insulted because of the name of Christ, you are blessed for the Spirit of glory and of God rests on you."* (1 Peter 4:14)

Often I forget how easy I have it in the United States. There are countries where Christians are beaten, tortured, and killed because of their faith...even the leaders of these countries are threatened by the power of Jesus. I have the privilege to share my faith with anyone, worship Jesus anywhere, and even relate my school work to my beliefs. And I have learned, through the Word and power of God, that character is highly esteemed. Good character and great knowledge are obtained by living a life worthy of the Lord!

From our readers...

— A mature Christian cannot be measured chronologically. How I wish I were more like her. I am humbled by her words.

Joy and Laughter

May God bless you this day...and may you laugh...a lot!

It was a dark and stormy night.

Well, OK. It wasn't stormy, but it was dark. The kind of dark you find at night. The kind of night when strange and mysterious things happen. Beverly and I had gone to bed after working hard all day. We were exhausted and sleep came quickly.

Then suddenly, in the middle of that dark and mysterious night, Beverly woke up. Something, some noise had roused her from a deep sleep. She glanced at the clock. Her eyes slowly focused on 3:00 a.m. Then there was that noise again. There was someone in the room. Someone walking...pacing actually...back and forth...back and forth. Startled she reached for me, but I wasn't there. She looked closer at the pacing image. With her eyes quickly adjusting to the dim light, she finally recognized the lonely figure, with head bent downward, still pacing back and forth. It was her beloved husband...me.

"Chuck? What are you doing?" she asked, obviously overcome with worry at the sight of me equally overcome with some grave concern that had me up in the middle of the dark and mysterious night.

Without hesitation...without even raising my head or even slowing my pace...I firmly replied, "I'm looking for the lawn mower."

It was, of course, at that precise moment, having heard my own words...that I woke up.

What followed was very loud, maniacal laughter that continued for what seemed several hours. It would be incorrect to say that Beverly was merely laughing hard or that tears were rolling down her cheeks. That would be true, but hardly a sufficient description. Suffice it to say that it was impossible to have any intelligent conversation with her for quite some time, or even for her to seriously consider my explanations or that perhaps she had misunderstood me when I said that I was looking at the "wrong door"…because I had been thinking about changing the doors in the house…sometime…possibly. No use. She never heard a word.

When I was younger, I took everything very seriously, especially myself. I never laughed at my mistakes. Every error seemed magnified in my eyes as I desperately sought perfection in everything I did. This made me at times a fairly unforgiving, intolerant and unmerciful person. And that was not what God wanted. His desire was that my life show *"love, joy, peace, patience, kindness, goodness, faithfulness, gentleness and self-control."* (Galatians 5:22-23)

I believe whenever God gives us such a list, He places them in that order for a reason. I can love others by doing things to help them. But I can't have patience, kindness, goodness, faithfulness, gentleness or self-control if I have no joy. I certainly cannot have peace. And how can I have joy if I take myself so seriously, if I cannot join in the laughter of others when I go looking for my lawn mower?

Paul once said, *"Rejoice in the Lord always. I will say it again: Rejoice! Let your gentleness be evident to all…And the peace of God, which transcends all understanding, will guard your hearts and your minds in Christ Jesus."* (Philippians 1:4-7) He also recognized the importance of having joy.

This week as you deal with the reality of life, laugh as much as you can, especially at yourself. You'll be amazed at how such a simple act will endear you to others, make you more real and therefore more accessible to them, and begin relationships that can last a lifetime. And always remember, if on some dark and mysterious night you find yourself pacing in your bedroom and someone asks you what you're doing, do <u>NOT</u> say you're looking for the lawn mower.

Take care and be God's.

From our readers...

— Isn't it funny how we remember the odd things people do but sometimes it is hard to recall the big things? Perhaps that keeps us "human" and allows others to relate to us.

— Thanks for the Note. It reminds me I still take things too serious. Also, I really need to laugh more.

Renewed Devotion

May God bless you this day...with renewed devotion!

Be devoted to one another in brotherly love. Honor one another above yourselves. Romans 12:10

I began to understand the Bible more when it dawned on me that it is not a history book filled with do's and don'ts. While there is much history and instruction, the real importance of the Bible comes from the fact that, at its very heart, it is a book about relationships. My relationship with God and His relationship with me. My relationship with Jesus and the Holy Spirit. My relationship with other people, those I dislike, those I like, enemies, friends, relatives. My relationship with other Christians.

As I've studied what the Bible says about relationships, I frequently encounter a concept often ignored in our culture today: Devotion. Oh, sure, we are called to be devoted to God, the teachings of Christ, and the leading of the Holy Spirit. We hear plenty about those, but what about devotion to each other within the Body of Christ? What about devotion from one Christian to another, and back again?

"What is devotion?" Well, I'm glad you asked. Devotion is defined as 'ardent attachment or loyalty'. "And that means...what?" OK, ardent means 'marked by a sincere and deeply held adoring love'; attachment or loyalty is 'a bond of faithfulness held intensely or personally'; and faithfulness is that state of 'being firmly supportive, trustworthy, and reliable'. Putting it all together, devotion is:

A sincere and deeply held adoring love which creates an intense, personal bond characterized by firm mutual support, trust, and reliability.

One of the things that strikes me about this is that devotion must be <u>personally</u> held. If it is to be true and lasting, devotion cannot be demanded or wished for. King David tried that when he ordered his people to be devoted to God and when he prayed that God would give his son devotion. (1 Chronicles 22:19; 29:19) But as David himself acknowledged, God searches every heart and understands every motive behind the thoughts (1 Chronicles 28:9), and He knows when it's a sham. Devotion must come from within.

This idea of devotion is especially important to Christians today. Take a look around and you'll see people hurting and struggling everywhere. And in the midst of all this, what do we do when we see a Christian brother or sister in need? Do we try to comfort them by our presence and prayers? Do we support them...emotionally, physically and financially...through their difficulties? Can we be trusted in this relationship? Are we reliable? Do we really care?

Sometimes the only support we are willing to give is prayer and the only expense we are willing to part with is the brief amount of time and effort we spend in prayer. Sincere prayer is powerful, but it is not the only thing we can do. Remember that the early Church was devoted not only to prayer, but also to the fellowship. *"All the believers were together and had everything in common. Selling their possessions and goods, they gave to anyone as he had need."* (Acts 2:44-45) They gave action with their prayers.

In his time of need, Job said, *"A despairing man should have the devotion of his friends, even though he forsakes the fear of the Almighty. But my brothers are as undependable as intermittent streams..."* (Job 6:14-15) Are we dependable or, as God said of the Israelites, is our devotion nothing but words? (Ezekiel 33:31) When you think about it, devotion is nothing more...and nothing less...than loving one another.

Take care and be God's.

From our readers...

— *I went into McDonald's to acquire a soda to drink and was behind a lady that appeared to be in her late 60's. The Holy Spirit convicted me that I should pray for her, with her and over her. When she was ordering I noticed she sounded a bit curt and felt she could do with some instruction in manners. Upon her receipt of her order, I wished her a blessed day and felt I had done my duty. As I was placing the lid on my drink, I noticed she was having a tough time with her shake and offered to retrieve her spoon, which I did.*

I decided that I had done my good deed and that it was time to make my exit. I proceeded to drive out of the parking lot, all the while convincing myself that I would simply just pray for her, that I didn't have to do it in her presence. The Holy Spirit simply would not let go even though I said my prayer. I turned around and went back, (forget that I was on my way to the school tennis match.) Upon entering McDonald's, I found the lady there and proceeded to ask her to pardon my interrupting her shake, but that I felt convicted by the Holy Spirit to pray with her. She gave me a brief story...

She has been battling manic depression for years and there was a recent discovery of a large mass in her right breast. She was to go see the cancer doctor on the following Thursday. Her sister died at 56 from breast cancer! She truly appreciated the prayer for her and her son whom she lives with. She has the bottom floor and he the top.

I was way out of my comfort zone, and had been really arguing with the Holy Spirit about praying for and with a total stranger. But God showed me 2 things – her hairs are numbered just like mine and that our comfort zone doesn't matter, just our obedience to Him. The Holy Spirit had also brought to mind the fact that when we shun the Holy Spirit's direction, we head toward a hardened heart, something we should run from as Christians.

— Thanks for that word. I forwarded that to the men's group at our church, because devotion perfectly describes what I've experienced with those men in the past two weeks. Two weeks ago tomorrow a brother of ours took his own life, for reasons we will never know this side of heaven...Hearing the news later that day shook me to my core, and as we gathered the following Wednesday night and shared our memories and our own struggles, I experienced the devotion that you describe. And I know that his widow, children and family have experienced that devotion, too.

The Desires of Your Heart

May God bless you this day...and grant you the desires of your heart!

God has blessed me in some amazing ways! One of the things I get to do is to counsel and advise churches, ministries and missions, helping them in their efforts to carry out God's work. This is definitely a blessing that works both ways. The more times God allows me to use my gifts, talents, and skills to bless others, the more He uses those same people to bless me in return. One winter day I was summoned to the home of some friends in Colorado. Over the better part of four days, we talked about a tremendous ministry opportunity, truly a Spirit-filled and Spirit-led effort. I helped guide some of the discussion, offered some ideas about strategy, and gave another perspective on issues of planning, focus, and organization. Throughout our meetings, two statements kept coming to the table. The first served as a constant reminder of 'Who' is really in charge: "We have to make sure that whatever we do is in agreement with God's will, in line with His timing, and in keeping with His direction." The second always closely followed the first: "And He will give us the desires of our hearts in a way and to a depth we could never have imagined."

What an incredible idea! If we are totally committed to God, working hard to follow Him and do the work He has laid out, He will look into the far reaches of our hearts and give us what we so desperately want. Sound too good to be true? Just look at this.

Delight yourself in the Lord and He will give you the desires of your heart. Psalms 37:4

Do you know how to "delight yourself in the Lord"?

The Bible tells us how we approach this: Trust in God... Commit your way to Him...Wait for His leading...Keep to His plans...Keep the peace...Study His word and learn Who He is...Obey His commands...Do good to others. When we do these things, He transforms us into the people He has called us to be. Our hopes and dreams come in line with His.

We can look to God, express our deepest desires, and not feel ashamed or selfish because we know that above all, we want His will to rule our lives. It's no longer "our plans", but "God's purpose". No longer a "self-serving wish", but a "Godly desire". We're talking here about the deep desires of every person who truly loves and follows Christ...the desires that bring honor, glorify and praise to His name.

My friends were great examples of this. They had long desired that God would grant them a cabin in the woods which could be used for His work. What He gave them was an awesome home in the wonders of the Colorado Rockies, where men and women on the front lines of ministry can come and find refuge in the love of God expressed through the hearts of my friends. God gave them the true desires of their hearts and He did it in a marvelous way they could never have foreseen and to an extent they could never have imagined. Our God is an awesome God!

After long days of intense discussions and fervent prayers, I left Colorado to return to my home in Georgia. During the flight, I thought about these things. What are the desires of <u>my</u> heart that would make God happy? Could I ever be so blessed that He would give them to me? Is all of this really true or just wishful thinking? And then it suddenly dawned on me. I looked to the seat next to me and there slept my wife, who had accompanied me on this long trip. She had gone with no expectation of participating. She just wanted to be with me. She is the love of my life...my greatest companion, supporter, encourager, and friend. And she is without doubt one of the greatest desires my heart has ever had. And that day...March 18...on which we had a cancelled flight, missed our connection, suffered through 9 hours of delays, spent a long day in airports and a night on a plane, and then finally made it home at 3:30 in the morning...that day marked the 23rd anniversary of when God gave me the desire of my heart.

It's true! He does give us the desires of our heart. Let God mold you into the person He wants you to be, tell Him your deepest desires, and watch as our Heavenly Father shows you His incredible love.

Take care and be God's.

From our readers...

— Isn't it amazing that the true desires of our hearts are already here...You know I read something last week that I need to be reminded of often especially since I am a planner. "If you are always planning for tomorrow and thinking about the past, you never live in the present."

— Just wanted you to know, I am in the process of study and prayer prior to entering the ministry. This Note struck me exactly where I am, and changed my perspective of a small problem. I was not delighting in the Lord, but worrying how "I" was going to make ends meet rather than turning it over to God's Will. I enjoy and look forward to each week's note as it always lifts my spirit and brightens my week.

— Having moved a mere 27 times throughout our military life, we had it down to a science. Everything gets packed, if it hasn't been unpacked since the last move, then it gets pitched. Then we all sit down and write a list of things we

want God to do for us at our new location. What type of house, how big, what particulars we would like. As we told the kids, God already knows what we NEED, what we were asking for were things we WANTED. God always came through and usually added His own special touch. He is such an awesome God, so caring and loving, I can't imagine my life without Him.

Pay Attention and Listen

May God bless you this day…as you listen to Him!

I have a hearing problem that requires me to be careful about what I think I hear. Once a friend and I were in a restaurant, a setting that's often hard for me because the background noise confuses the signals going to my brain. Instead of hearing words, I just hear more noise. This day I was having a difficult time understanding what my friend was saying, but I did hear something concerning a youth musical he was very excited about. Then he told me the name. I was shocked. How could anyone, much less a church group, name a youth musical *that*? Then I remembered, "Chuck, you don't hear so good", and I asked him to repeat it. The name of the musical was "Bright New Wings." Well, that made ever so much more sense than "Breaking Wind".

It is very important to "PAY ATTENTION!" Just hearing words is not enough. We have to listen carefully to what is being said, think about it, understand it. Many of us fail to listen. We get so caught up with giving our solution, we fail to understand the problem. Or we just assume what's going on, and then miss everything completely. Like when we read the Bible. For example, we know that…

> *The idols of the nations are silver and gold, made by the hands of men. They have mouths, but cannot speak, eyes, but they cannot see; they have ears, but cannot hear, nor is there breath in their mouths. Those who make them will be like them…* Psalms 135:15-18

But we fail to listen to the rest: *and so will all who trust in them.*

Without listening to what God tells us, we cannot

understand Him! It's easy to point to those who manufacture the objects of man's desires and constantly encourage us to buy whatever it is they're selling, but what about us, the consumers? Have we put our trust in those objects? Be honest. Where is our trust really? Is it in a job, a house, or a car? What about our checking account, retirement plan, or stock portfolio? Or can we, like the Psalmist who did not look to power, wealth or possessions, say with all confidence, *"I trust in the name of the LORD my God!"* (Psalms 20:7) Here's a test: If you lost it all, would you still trust God?

And why is this important? PAY ATTENTION! Because if we actually trust in the things made by man, <u>we will be like them</u> — we will have mouths but cannot speak, eyes but cannot see, and ears but cannot hear. God's Word will become nothing more than advice; His miracles, just stories; and His voice, meaningless noise. We will comprehend nothing, failing to understand something important about the only path to eternity:

This is my command: Love each other. John 15:17

If you love me, you will obey what I command. John 14:15

He who does not love me will not obey my teaching. John 14:24a

Do not merely listen to the word, and so deceive yourselves. Do what it says. James 1:22

...faith by itself, if it is not accompanied by action, is dead. James 2:17

Not everyone who says to me, "Lord, Lord," will

enter the kingdom of heaven, but only he who does the will of my Father who is in heaven. Matthew 7:21

When it comes to you and the object of your trust, is it a *what* or a *who*? And when you hear God whisper, *"Whoever claims to live in Him must walk as Jesus did,"* (1 John 2:6), do you understand what He's telling you or is it just a lot of noise?

Pay attention. Listen carefully. Seek God's understanding with everything you've got. Eternity with Him hangs in the balance.

Take care and be God's.

From our readers...

— *Reminds me of the verse, "Be still and know that I am God." Emphasis on the "Be Still" part. I get so busy sometimes that I fail to be quiet and listen to Him.*

— *Sometimes we hear what we want to.*

Test Everything

**May God bless you this day…and when you test
a new way!**

*Do not put out the Spirit's fire; do not treat
prophecies with contempt. Test everything. Hold on
to the good.* 1 Thessalonians 5:19-22

Not every new idea that comes along is a good one. For some strange reason, we try to reinvent the wheel, come up with that new and exciting approach. And bigger just looks so much better.

When I was in college, I was a member of Alpha Phi Omega, a service fraternity more like the Robin Hoods of campus. We had no house and our parties usually stunk, but we had a good time helping others. And, of course, we did have our hallowed ritual of "The Flaming Arrow". As our leader would reach a certain point in the initiation ceremony, a signal would be secretly given. Then, a hundred yards away, a flaming arrow would be shot through the night sky, landing safely in a nearby river. The only problem was that it never worked. We would carefully light the arrow, the designated archer would draw back on the bow, and then the flame would disappear about 2 feet into flight. Every year our best effort amounted to little more than a brief flare up, the swish of an invisible arrow, and the sound of a distant splash as it hit the water. It was always memorable to the new members simply because it can be a frightening thing when you realize an arrow has been shot but you don't know where it's headed.

Then one year I came up with an idea. A bigger and better idea. If a flaming arrow wouldn't work, what about a flaming spear? The flame would be larger and since we couldn't throw it as fast as a speeding arrow, surely it wouldn't go out. My fellow brothers foolishly agreed. Bigger would be better. So we took an old broom handle and tightly tied a knot of rags at the end. Then, just to make sure it would flame up real good, we soaked it in kerosene...for two days. Yep. Two whole days.

The night of the initiation came and, since it was my brilliant idea, I was selected to be the official spear flinger. We carefully took our pride and joy, found a suitable hiding place, and waited. That night the sky was overcast, and except for the flowing river, there were no sounds at all. It was as if the birds, bullfrogs, and crickets somehow knew what was about to unfold. In fact, I'm convinced they had called their friends, quickly built a large grandstand, and were silently sitting in the dark eating their popcorn.

The ceremony began. We tensed with excitement as the opening words were spoken. Then came the secret signal. I grabbed the holy spear in one hand and got myself into proper flinging position while my three partners each proceeded to light it. What happened next we know mainly from piecing together various accounts.

The big spear, unlike the little arrow, did not simply ignite. Instead, it literally <u>burst</u> into flames and I suddenly found myself holding a broom handle with a sizeable fireball on the end. It was at that moment that my friends and I screamed in unison. Not wanting to have the growing fireball anywhere near me, I quickly flung it into the blackness of the night, which, of course, was fairly well lit up at the moment. And our great experiment came to an end...that is, it would have...had the stupid thing not lodged in the top of a tree leaning out over the river. I can still hear one brother making rather rude comments about my idea as he inched his way out onto a limb to retrieve the still burning spear, which was then unceremoniously dumped into the water below. A few weeks later, after my eyebrows had grown back, I conceded that perhaps it would have been good to have actually tested my idea before jumping to the conclusion that this was the "great new way".

That turns out to be a pretty good rule for just about anything and I've tried to remember it whenever I get excited about every new thing that comes along...especially "new" teaching. We hear new ideas and insights all the time, some designed only to satisfy what our itching ears want to hear. But regardless of where or whom they come from, we have to test them against what we know to be true. Bigger isn't always better. When it comes to how Christians should live, what we believe, and even how we worship, every new idea should be able to stand with what Jesus has already said. Even Paul had to go through this.

Now the Bereans were of more noble character than the Thessalonians, for they received the message with great eagerness and examined the Scriptures every day to see if what Paul said was true. Acts 17:11

Think, wonder and dream. Don't be afraid to try something new, but test everything against the Word of God. It will help keep us all on the right path...and you'll hang on to your eyebrows longer.

Take care and be God's.

The Purpose of Prayer

May God bless you this day…as you pray!

Trouble comes in different ways…sickness, injury, and death…lost jobs and careers…shattered hopes and dreams… betrayal and broken promises…difficult tasks and responsibilities. We can be left shaken, confused, frustrated, hurt, angry or afraid. And then what do we do? We pray. But what is prayer, and what's the point? If God already knows what's going to happen, why pray at all?

Prayer is defined in two significantly different ways. First, it may be a reverent petition or request made to God. OK, that's easy, but this doesn't really tell us the point of prayer…the "why" behind the doing. We can always fall back on the "Because God told us to" approach, but that's hardly satisfying and does little to help us grow in our spiritual understanding.

It's like driving a car in a storm. I go down a road and a terrible storm overtakes me with heavy rain and strong winds. I've been told to grip the steering wheel more firmly, and so I do. By doing that, I stay on course. We all instinctively grip the wheel better in those situations because we understand why. If we don't, we'll be blown off the road. But what if we didn't understand the need, the "why" behind it all? Would we still grip the wheel as tightly? While you're thinking about that, consider this. Every time you drive a car, there is the possibility a tire will blow out, jerking you into the path of an oncoming car. Do you <u>always</u> hold the wheel firmly with two hands? Today many people get flat tires, but few ever have a real blowout. Without the understanding, we can be careless about the instruction to hold the wheel firmly.

It's the same with prayer. It isn't enough to simply know what prayer is. We also need to understand the purpose behind prayer. The second definition helps in this respect: Prayer is an act of communion with God. And what is communion? "An act or instance of sharing; a religious or spiritual fellowship."

Throughout the Bible, we are instructed to pray and through prayer to present our requests to God. But prayer is not the "asking". As Jesus taught in His Model Prayer (Matthew 6:9-13), prayer is the "time of fellowship" between us and God in which we recognize (1) who God is, (2) who we are in relation to Him, and (3) who we are in relation to others. But if God already knows what's going to happen, why should we pray? I've come up with something that may help here:

Prayer is the means by which God draws back the curtains of our minds, allowing us to look through a window of love so that we may see Him and know what He is doing.

By devoting ourselves to prayer, being watchful and thankful (Colossians 4:2), and praying on all occasions with all kinds of prayers and requests (Ephesians 6:18), God gives us more and more opportunities to see Him at work and, by doing so, to better understand who He is. Through this "spiritual communion", we draw closer to God and He draws closer to us, strengthening our relationship. We pray because God wants to show us how much He loves us. And through our shared experiences, He shows us how to pray correctly, which just makes the relationship that much stronger.

Think about it. Suppose someone asks you to pray about a stranger's illness. Later you learn of that person's miraculous and complete recovery. How would it make you feel? Would it reaffirm that God still exists, that He hears you when you pray, that He cares? Would you feel a little closer to Him, a little surer of Him, and a little safer with Him than before? God may have healed the stranger...but He answered you!

Maybe now some of those hard commands like *"pray for those who mistreat you"* (Luke 6:28) make a little more sense. The praying isn't so much about the other person or that situation. It's about our relationship with God and the people we can become...as we grip the wheel firmly and stay on course.

Take care and be God's.

From our readers...

— I find it remarkable that, once again, you have "hit MY nail" squarely on the head...Thank you, again, for another uncannily-timely message to meet my needs.

Share Your Prayer

May God bless you this day...through prayer.

Do we really believe in prayer? Or do we just not take advantage of the opportunity? Those in the early Church were devoted to the apostles' teaching, fellowship, breaking of bread, and prayer. And what did this accomplish? *"Everyone was filled with awe, and many wonders and miraculous signs were done by the apostles."* (*see* Acts 2:42-47) But what did they pray about? Well, Paul tells us to pray *"on all occasions with all kinds of prayers and requests."* (Ephesians 6:18)

Then why don't we? When we're sick, hurting, depressed, out of work, or all sorts of other terrible things happen to us, why don't we rush to ask others to pray for us? Throughout his letters, even Paul specifically asked for prayer for himself. What prevents so many of us from doing the same?

Sometimes it's pride. We just can't admit we're in trouble. At times, it's fear. By asking for prayer, we have to admit that the problem is real. And at other times it's a lack of faith. The problem seems so big we don't want to risk God not answering it. "What if He doesn't get me a new job..." "What if He doesn't heal me..." "What if my spouse divorces me anyway..." "What if..." We don't understand the real purpose of prayer, and deep inside we're afraid that what we see as "no answer" means that God is angry with us...He's too busy...our problems are too small...or maybe He doesn't really exist after all.

There are many reasons why we are told to pray, but one seems to be overlooked or even ignored on a fairly consistent basis...even by leaders of the Church. Over and over we are told to love and encourage each other and to seek unity in the Church. There is no better way than by praying with and for each other. Through prayer we learn of needs, fears, concerns, hopes and dreams. We share in each other's joy and elation as well as grief and sorrow. Simply put, we become the family God has called us to be.

But though we've been told, even commanded, to pray for others, we often fail to share our own prayer requests. And I have to admit I'm one of the worst. You see, autoimmune diseases tend to run in my family and I have this real cute one that causes my body to produce tiny blood clots all the time. It isn't life-threatening, thankfully, but mornings can be miserable experiences. You know how you feel achy all over when you have the flu real bad? Welcome to my world. For most mornings, that makes it literally a real "pain" to get up early and attend any meeting before about 9 a.m.

But do I ask for prayer? Nooooo. And that's dumb because even if I wake up hurting again tomorrow, I have denied someone a great opportunity today. I have prevented them from being a part of my life. I have kept them at arm's length and established between us a barrier. I have denied them the chance to express to God how they feel, which in turn can help them. But more importantly, I have made it very hard for us to be "family". Imagine what happens when we all do that.

Learn to open up. Find some people you can share with, who will pray for you and will allow you to pray for them. There's a lot of garbage going on in the world and we need each other right now. And if you don't have anyone at this particular time, lean on us. We're here. We will pray with and for you. And I hope you will pray for us and this ministry. And, oh yeah, by the way, I'd appreciate the prayers, too. Mornings can be bad.

Take care and be God's.

From our readers...

— *But besides pride, lack of faith and fear of reality, there
is another reason we don't pray enough...fear of intimacy.
Prayer is the most intimate moment we have with God.
There are those of us that have a hard enough time developing relationships anyway. Our relationship with God is
no exception. Opening ourselves up to the kind of scrutiny
that comes with intimacy is not a comfortable prospect. As
a result, I tend to keep a bit of distance between me and
most everyone else, even God. Academically, I know God
knows me more intimately than anyone else and there is
nothing I can hide from Him. Nonetheless, it's still difficult
to open up and "give it up". I'm doing better today than
yesterday, which is better than the day before, which is
better.....*

— *We definitely don't pray enough. We rob others of experiencing God's blessing.*

— *My husband tells me how he feels and yet, I find it difficult (like you) to mention how I feel. Like what a bad time I
had walking across the parking lot this morning with my
knee, or walking into the kitchen with my feet...I feel like I
sound like a broken record.. But If I don't mention it then
everyone thinks I am OK.*

Death on the Appalachian Trail

May God bless you this day…as you show Him to others!

We know that we have passed from death to life,
because we love our brothers. Anyone who does not
love remains in death. 1 John 3:14

I love backpacking and hiking, which I've been doing for many years now. I never get tired of walking through the dense forests, climbing mountains, discovering waterfalls and streams, and seeing those views you just can't capture on film. I'm never closer to God than when I'm walking with Him in this incredible world He's created. I also enjoy meeting the many different people there. Few backpackers really know each other, but they recognize the trail names. Like Nomad, Mr. D, Jo Jo Smiley, Bandana, and one of my favorites, Screaming Knees. My own is Stryder, spelled that way partly because on the trail my motto is *In everything 'try'*. Cute, huh?

A few years ago I was introducing a friend to the Appalachian Trail and took him up to Springer Mountain, the southern beginning point. It was a great day for hiking. The sun was out, the sky was clear and blue, and it was nice and cool. We had a great start, walking beside babbling brooks, through fern covered hillsides, and just really enjoying life on the trail. And then it happened.

We had just left a beautiful area called Three Forks and were into a long climb, when we saw a man running down the trail toward us. He yelled out that he and his friends had just found a guy in trouble who needed medical help. After I directed him to Three Forks where he might find someone with a cell phone or radio, my friend and I hurried on. When we arrived, three men were standing near the trail and one was lying on the ground. But that guy was no longer in trouble. He had died, as we discovered later, from a massive aneurysm.

The three men standing by had hiked with this man earlier in the day, but as they rested at Three Forks, he had ventured on alone. Now in shock, they couldn't bring themselves to admit the poor man was dead. It fell on me to confirm it. I've done a fair amount of Christian counseling over the years, and I found myself doing a good bit right then. There was denial, grief, disbelief, even anger. It's strange how we react sometimes when tragedy strikes. One of the men kept repeating, "This can't be happening. I just talked to him two hours ago."

There are no promises when it comes to how long any of us live. We could last for 100 years or die tomorrow. Some may see death waiting around a corner, while others never see it coming. All the more reason for us to understand that every moment of life is precious, a time to cherish and use wisely. But it's not only for ourselves. Every day there are countless times we can let others see the love of Christ in our lives. Relatives, friends, business associates, neighbors. People we work and socialize with; those we encounter throughout the day. Many need to experience God's love, some for the very first time. And they need to experience it through us. But like us, their time in this world is running out...and they may have no more chances. Their clock is ticking and every day is another day gone.

Look around and watch the people God brings across your path. Smile. Be friendly. Take the opportunity to let them know you care. Like that man on the trail, they may not have a tomorrow. Let them experience God in your life. You may be their last chance to know Him.

Take care and be God's.

From our readers…

— Your Note hit home today because I had been thinking of the death of a friend of mine this morning and what a shock it was…You know as I get older, I am more aware of the shortness of my time. I guess that is one reason I want to make changes in my life. This may sound morbid but it's not meant to be, just the facts…The bottom line is that there are lots of things that I would like to do that are more important than my job.

— I needed this one even today…I should live each day as if it were my last and stop wasting so much time dwelling on unimportant problems.

We're At War

May God bless you this day...as you prepare for war!

I looked for a man among them who would build up the wall and stand before me in the gap on behalf of the land so I would not have to destroy it, but I found none. Ezekiel 22:30

One week I took a long-needed break and went to a calm place where I could watch endless waves, walk along a sandy shore, and talk with God. I thought about this ministry and the many I'm privileged to work with and help. And I asked Him a few questions.

— *"What's it all for? A few seem to listen, but many don't. In fact, they choose not to. What's the point?"*

— *"Pay attention and understand,"* He whispered.

One day I saw some relatives I hadn't seen in far too long. There were hugs, laughter, and stories to tell. But there was one image in all of that, like a photograph in time, that especially stood out. On November 21, 1970, a new Graham was welcomed into the family. She was small, fragile, and she was a, well, a "she". Not only the first baby in a while, but also the first baby "girl" in about 18 years. But the best part was that this new little Graham was the first baby I ever held. That week I saw this baby again. She got out of the car and stood up, all while chattering away (she's got Graham blood, remember). Then she reached back into the car and lifted into her arms...her own little baby girl.

— *"So, is this it, God? Children, new people, one generation to the next? Is this the point?"*

— *"Partly. But you're still talking. Pay attention and understand."*

Throughout the week, there were calls for help. A family struggled with the news their son has returned to drugs. A church was in upheaval and there was dissension in the staff. A pastor faced a possible call for his resignation. A student missionary was shocked by the number of teenage pregnancies, alcoholics and drug users in her area. Others shared of problems at work, losing work, and finding work.

But these were not the cries of defeat. They were the shouts of victory as they reached out, shared their struggles, spoke of their pain, and asked for prayer. Victory through the hope they had in the One who loves them. And they even had thanks. Yes, thanks for remembering, for not letting them feel so alone.

— *"So we're to just keep on keeping on because every-one needs somebody sometime?"*

— *"It's more than that. Pay attention and understand."*

I remember on June 7, 2002, Philippine soldiers raided an outpost of the Muslim terrorists, Abu Sayyaf. Martin Burnham...missionary of New Tribes Mission, husband of Gracia, father of Jeff, Mindy and Zach, son of Paul and Oreta (also missionaries), brother of Doug, hostage for more than a year, but always a man devoted to God...was killed. His wife escaped. It had almost been a year since the only other American kidnapped, Guillermo Sobero, had been beheaded. And on Sunday, June 9, Christians went about their daily routines, as though nothing had happened.

— *"Oh, I understand. We're at war."*

Many years ago Moses and Joshua descended Mt. Sinai and heard a great noise. Not realizing the Israelites were worshipping a golden calf, Joshua said, "There is the sound of war in the camp." But Moses replied, *"It is not the sound of the cry of triumph, nor is it the sound of the cry of defeat; but the sound of singing I hear."* (Exodus 32:17-18) Moses understood. No cry of triumph. No cry of defeat. Just singing...for nothing. The people failed to understand there was a war going on.

There is a war going on all around us. It is spiritual and

it is deadly. Sometimes the attack comes from without, such as with Martin Burnham. More often, the attacks come from within. Christians assail Christians. Churches become weak. Denominations implode. But if we could just understand that we're in a war with very real casualties, perhaps we'd be more forgiving, loving, understanding, and devoted to each other, and less judgmental, arrogant, demanding, and focused on our own wisdom.

We all need more encouragement if we're to get through this war. Adults need it. Children need it. And their children will need it, too. Encouragement is important. Pay attention and understand — *I am a man of peace; but when I speak, they are for war.* (Psalms 120:7)

Take care and be God's.

From our readers...

— I believe the problem begins with the way witnessing and preaching are done. People are always touting up the kingdom of heaven and the wonderful blessings in store for the converted. Instead, we should look at it as recruiting for war time military duty. Just as in the military, not all Christians will be called upon to be on the front lines, but each and every member of the military is vitally important to the mission.

While I know the Lord has blessed me and my family much more than we deserve, not everyone would see our situation as a blessing. But over the years I have learned to change the perspective in the way I view the daily events in our lives. Now it is much easier to see God's Hand in our lives and I am thankful to say that our children have also learned to view our circumstances in a good light.

— I'm a woman pastor in rural Georgia. I just wanted to take the time to let you know I read your Notes and I appreciate them greatly. But tonight as I read this one, I too have asked the Lord why this ministry. I see Christians who once they get what they want from the Lord, they tend to become too busy to help the child that no one wants, or just don't have the time for the family that is falling apart. But tonight, you have indeed encouraged me to keep on, for all the ones who are thought about.

When You Enter the Battle

May God bless you this day...as you enter the battle.

I work with many churches, missions, and ministries, and I see a lot of frustration. A pastor struggles for Christian integrity in Atlanta. A missionary reaches into Muslim villages in Africa. A minister meets resistance to sharing the Gospel in Russia. A tired Christian band shares God's message one more time. An undermanned mission tries to feed, clothe and shelter the poor. A restless congregation starves for the truth of God's Word. A lonely pulpit looks out into a sea of vacant expressions from those who have eyes but do not see and ears but do not hear.

There are battles with governments, agencies, and individuals throughout the world...a world that labors long and hard in its fight against God. And frustrations are not limited to such obvious arenas. They arise all around us. Encounters with angry bosses and inept employees, problems with bills that overcharge and bills that go unpaid, nursing homes that fail to provide proper care...and the list goes on and on. We want to do good in these situations. We want to do the "Christ" thing. But the more we try, the more we get hit in the face. Many of us may not be in a foreign mission field or heading up a ministry effort, but our faith gets challenged every day. And often in ways so subtle we forget that our Christian witness is on the line.

Frustration leads to disappointment. Disappointment gives way to anger. Anger creates depression. And depression lays the foundation for lost hope, confusion, fear, and eventually...defeat.

This **Note** is not going to give you some man-made 12 step program for how to find happiness. Those are often meant to sell books. Nor will you find the easy "cure". I will leave that to the marketing people behind all the diets of the world. Instead, regardless of who you are or what your calling in life may be, let's focus on something really radical in today's world...the truth.

<u>Why do these things happen to me</u>?

...you do not belong to the world, but I have chosen you out of the world. That is why the world hates you...If they persecuted me, they <u>will</u> persecute you also...They will treat you this way because of my name, for they do not know the One who sent me. John 15:18-22

<u>Can't I just get along?</u>

...Anyone who chooses to be a friend of the world becomes an enemy of God. James 4:4

<u>Then who is this fight against</u>?

For our struggle is not against flesh and blood, but against the rulers, against the authorities, against the powers of this dark world and against the spiritual forces of evil in the heavenly realms. Ephesians 6:12

<u>What should I do</u>?

...be strong in the Lord and in His mighty power... take your stand against the devil's schemes...put on the full armor of God, so that when the day of evil comes, you may be able to stand your ground, and after you have done everything, to stand. Ephesians 6:10,11,13

And how do I do that?

Whoever claims to live in Him must walk as Jesus did.
1 John 2:6

What hope do I really have?

...the One who is in you is greater than the one who is in the world. 1 John 4:4

What does this mean to me personally...every day?

I can do everything through Him who gives me strength. Philemon 4:13

We are strangers in this world and it can be a very difficult place. My prayer is that at the end of the day we can say, "*I have fought the good fight, I have finished the race, I have kept the faith.*" (2 Timothy 4:7)
Take care and be God's.

From our readers...

— *I need reminding that the people I come in contact with daily, for the most part, are not Christian. It is easy to get disappointed in people when they do not behave in a Christ-like manner but then they do not know Him.*

— *I feel lifted up and ready to face the day, whatever it may bring. I will take these words with me through the day today and at the end of the day, hopefully I will be happy in my walk with the Lord and He may also be pleased with my effort to serve Him.*

— Sometimes we don't stop and think that we really are in the battle but with Christ we WIN!

God's Reinforcements *by Susan Paradise*

May God bless you this day...as you get reinforced!

There is a spiritual war being waged. But what are we to do when it strikes those around us — our neighbors, friends, and family? Do we have any responsibility, obligation or duty? And what about when we are the target? From where will our help come?

> *Two are better than one, because they have a good return for their work: If one falls down, his friend can help him up. But pity the man who falls and has no one to help him up!* Ecclesiastes 4:9-10

Pay attention and understand. Listen carefully to that gentle whisper when it tells you to act.

Take care and be God's.

"God's Reinforcements"

Recently I had a "real" Monday. My day began bad and quickly went downhill. It culminated late that night with a phone call informing me of some really painful news about someone I love very much. This news left me with feelings of betrayal, failure, disappointment, and guilt. My husband and daughter were out for the evening so I had to handle it alone. The next morning I faced an empty office. My usual "support" people were out of town or out of reach. As my mind replayed that phone call, the walls began to close in on me. I called out to God for help — I had no one to talk to and I needed to talk.

Then the phone rang. It was a friend from church. She was struggling with a decision she needed to make and had just decided to call and ask my opinion. It was such a relief to have someone to talk to and get my mind off my pain! Suddenly the other line rang. It was another friend, and he wanted to see how I was doing. I told him I would call him back and then returned to my first call. She talked for a while and said she would like me to pray with her about this decision. I agreed and then asked if I could share my difficult news so that she could also join me in prayer.

After hearing my heartbreaking story, she immediately began sympathizing with and encouraging me. I told her how I had cried out to God for someone to talk to and then…she had called. She was excited that God would use her to help one of His hurting children and said she was as blessed as I was. She then led us in prayer and we hung up.

Feeling much better, I returned the second call. My friend could tell something was wrong, so I told him my news. He, too, immediately sympathized with and encouraged me. He shared that he had also lived through the same kind of grief and pain I was experiencing. He understood. And I could tell that it made him glad to use his own terrible experiences as a means of helping me in mine.

Chuck has often written about spiritual warfare. This week I wanted to share something of the hope we have in that warfare. God loves us so much that He sends "reinforcements" in the midst of the battles. These reinforcements, sometimes without even realizing it, become the instruments through which God strengthens us, helping us to stand in the face of betrayal, failure, disappointment, and even guilt. But the blessing isn't just to the one in need. It is also for the reinforcements — encouraging and strengthening those He chooses to use to encourage and strengthen others. It's a miracle, and each time this miracle is shared, the whole Army of God grows in power — His power. It's no wonder Who wins in the end!

From our readers...

— I have seen God meet my deepest needs over and over. His help almost always comes from some unexpected place or in an unexpected way. I believe that He does this so that I will have no doubt where it originated.

— Go and encourage others when God leads you too. Be obedient.

Stepping Up To The Plate

May God bless you this day...as you step up to the plate!

God likes to use His sense of humor to teach me lessons of life. When I was in the seventh grade, we played a lot of ball...baseball, softball, league, sandlot, organized, terribly unorganized. And once there were these two softball games with our biggest rival, played right after school on hot back-to-back spring afternoons. But it isn't the games I remember so well. It's how they ended.

In the first game, we were getting beat 6 to 4, but with two outs in the bottom of the last inning, we had managed to get the bases loaded. Then I stepped up to the plate. I can't tell you about the balls and strikes. I don't recall the look on the pitcher's face, the yells from my teammates, or the excitement in the stands. Well, yeah, I could tell you that because there were no stands. But what I do know is this — at some point I swung the bat really hard. I remember it leaving the infield like a cannon shot, landing deep in the outfield. I remember the guys on base moving instantly, racing to the next base and then home plate while I coasted into second. All runners had scored before the ball ever got back to the infield. We had won. And I remember feeling crushed by my teammates as they jumped on me in celebration. That had never happened to me before, and it was a great feeling. But the story doesn't end there.

The next day we played the second game, and it was almost a copy of the first. As the bottom of the last inning rolled around, we were getting beat again, this time 7 to 6. Runners were at second and third. Two outs. And...you guessed it...I'm called to the plate. Remembering the "blast", my teammates got excited, yelling for me to do it one more time. But I'd never had a game like the one before. I'd never been the hero. Now, suddenly, everyone "expected" me to come up with the hit that would save the day. Lots of pressure for a kid in the seventh grade, and I was very nervous. I swung at the first pitch and missed badly. Then came the second pitch. I swung again as hard as I could, but didn't even come close to the ball. I felt terrible, like I was letting everyone down. Then my coach yelled out, "Stop trying to kill the ball. Just be yourself and swing like you do in practice."

I calmed down and, as the third pitch floated in, swung evenly. This time I connected and drove the ball over the shortstop's head. Ah, but the outfielders, having learned from the day before, were positioned perfectly. The left fielder had been playing back and now came running hard toward the ball. Heading to first, I looked up and saw what was certain to be the final out of the game. But just then something unexpected happened. As the left fielder reached out to catch the ball, his over-sized cap (we wore what we could find back then) bounced off his head, landing perfectly upside down in his glove. An instant later the ball arrived and fell into the cap. The stunned boy watched helplessly as the ball and cap slid out of his glove before he could close it. We won. My team went nuts again, swarming me a second time.

As we were celebrating, I looked to the outfield. There was the guy who had dropped the ball, just sitting dejected and staring at the ground. Then one of his teammates ran over and patted him on the back, then another and another. I could hear them calling to him as they ran up, saying what a great "try" he'd made. Two grabbed him and lifted him to his feet, while the third handed him his cap and said, "Hey, you tried and that's what counts...but get rid of that cap!" Then they all laughed and trotted off the field.

You know, sometimes things work out the way we dream they would. Everything's perfect and there's that big happy ending. Other times things work out in spite of what we do, in ways we could never have expected. That's true in our Christian life as well, but even more so. When we commit to playing on God's team (bear with me here), He'll put us in the lineup. Sometimes we will use our gifts, talents, and abilities as He directs, and there will be success. Sometimes He will work His will through us and, in spite of our gifts, talents, and abilities, there will be success.

But even when it seems victory has slipped out of our grasp, He will still be there – personally and through our friends, our Christian "teammates" – to encourage us, lift our spirits, and prepare us for the next challenge. All we have to do is to make a real commitment to be on His team, let Him be the coach, step up to the plate and be prepared to do good as best we can. Then we can watch as the power and love of God explode through us, driving others home.

> *...we constantly pray for you, that our God may count you worthy of His calling, and that by His power He may fulfill every good purpose of yours and every act prompted by your faith. We pray this so that the name of our Lord Jesus may be glorified in you, and you in Him, according to the grace of our God and the Lord Jesus Christ.*
> 2 Thessalonians 1:11-12

Take care and be God's.

From our readers...

— Been there, done that on both offense and defense! Boy, how great I felt with the big save and how low when I blew it. It's really great to have a friend like Jesus who supports and loves us regardless of the successes but especially the failures.

— I know that this Note is written from the perspective of one who succeeds or fails and how he is treated by other people, but it also makes me think of my responsibility to others when I am one of those "other people."

Remembering…

The Dream of the King…for New Year's Day

May God bless you this day…and show you His dream.

What is God's plan for you? How has He chosen to use you this day…right now?

January 1 each year begins a unique season. A new year brings new beginnings and new resolutions. There are new diets, new promises, new hopes. Some years we have new government leaders with new goals and dreams. Not too long ago we even had a new millennium. It is definitely a time of change.

But I have a problem. You see, I really don't like change. Now I know many people who just can't get enough change in their lives. Every bend in the road is a new adventure, and that's great for them. But for me…well, change usually comes too quickly. I'd rather see things stay the same for a little while longer. Keep old friends around, rather than wave goodbye as they move away. Live in a nice community, rather than see every tree chopped down for yet another drug store. And play with my kids…while they're kids…rather than watch them grow up.

Change hit me a little harder one year. In 2000 my oldest son began his first year in college. He wasn't that far away, but my heart understood all too well that change had come. A change in life. A change in relationship. He was no longer my little boy. And it hurt whenever I thought about it too long.

Many years ago, a young man named Daniel lived an ordinary, routine life in ancient Israel. Nothing terribly unusual ever happened. Suddenly, without warning, his world changed. An army attacked his country. He was taken away from his family and friends, became a slave, and was forced to live in a strange land. Then one day the ruler of that land had a dream and called on Daniel to interpret it.

After hearing the dream, Daniel prayed and God showed him its meaning. Now, in all these things, Daniel was truly a victim of circumstances. He could have been very bitter about the severe and "unfair" changes in his life. He would have had excellent reasons for feeling that way. But he didn't complain. Instead, he praised God.

Praise be to the name of God for ever and ever; wisdom and power are His. He changes times and seasons; He sets up kings and deposes them. He gives wisdom to the wise and knowledge to the discerning. He reveals deep and hidden things; He knows what lies in darkness, and light dwells with Him. I thank and praise you, O God of my fathers: You have given me wisdom and power, you have made known to me what we asked of you, you have made known to us the dream of the king. Daniel 2:20-23

Every day brings change of one sort or another. Sometimes I have lingered in my misery, lost in the anxiety of the future while longing for the comfort of the past. But God – who allowed these changes – helps me to see them in a new way…His way. At the start of each day, I consciously renew my commitment to serve Him and follow Jesus. Now every bend in my road, every new direction, every change and every season…become new pages in the book God is writing for my life. And I'm never pushed along or left alone, because He is always with me…in front leading the way.

Serving Him, following Christ, and loving others…that is the dream of the King. Today, may you see the way to live His dream for you!

Take care and be God's.

From our readers...

— I have lupus and there is a lupus forum where God is using me to encourage others to stay focused on Jesus even when things are tough. God has redirected my life in the past three years in a direction I never would have believed He would. I have also been diagnosed with depression, anxiety disorder, AD/HD, fibromyalgia, and lupus, and all of this has taken place over the past three years, not to mention a devastating situation in my family that almost destroyed me. But because of the faith I have in my God, He has seen me through some very dark days. God is calling me to speak out to let other Christians know that just because one is battling their way through depression, it is not a lack of faith that has caused the depression. Depression is an illness in the brain that needs to be treated just like any other illness. Because of my faith and trust in God, He is now calling me to extend a hand out to other Christians to let them know depression is not caused by lack of faith.

— I needed this encouragement today. I too prefer things to change slowly, if at all. But I know the Lord has plans for my life and I must accept His will and go forward...I will be retiring soon. Another change. So I can only trust in the Lord to lead me from there as He does daily.

— I've heard for years that God is the same today, yesterday, and tomorrow. I used to want to say, "So what! What's the point!" That God doesn't change is one of the religious platitudes that I fuss about some, but I only really fuss when people spout a platitude like that when it doesn't have any real meaning to them. That God doesn't change is a big (sometimes even huge) source of comfort and security for me when my walls start to fall down and I begin to feel

helpless over all the change going on around me that I can't do anything about. The key is getting into the right mindset for this to become real to me. Sometimes I'm better at this than others.

The Act of Love...for Valentine's Day

May God bless you this day...as you love others!

Once upon a time I was teaching a Bible study on what it means to be a Christian. As is my style, I like to start off with something a little offbeat to get people's attention. So I decided I would ask a few in the class what they did for a living and then have them tell us how they would convince someone of that fact. As I was about to begin my lesson, I couldn't help laughing to myself about the perplexed faces I was about to see as a result of my clever plan. The first person I called on was a doctor, an anesthesiologist to be exact. You know, one of those who, like preachers, can put people to sleep while something really important is going on. I sat there, smiled, and asked, "So, what do you do for a living?" Without any pause or change of expression on his face, he calmly replied, "I pass gas."

Now, it is seldom that I am left completely speechless. However, at that moment, I have to admit my mind went totally blank. I pride myself in anticipating what others will say or do, but somehow in all of my planning, this possibility never arose. I just thank my Heavenly Father that I came to my senses long enough to change my strategy and not immediately demand, "Prove it."

February 14 in the U.S., as in a number of places around the world, is Valentine's Day. On this day people will exchange an assortment of cards, candy, and gifts as an expression of their love for each other. But more often than not, this "love", Human Love, refers to how we <u>feel</u> towards a person or thing. We use words and phrases like "endearing", "heartfelt", "a warm glow inside", and "that tingly feeling." But the "love" of the Bible, Godly Love, is something quite different. And the most basic differences are these:

Human Love is an emotion, feeling or attitude.

Godly Love transcends emotions, feelings and attitudes.

Human Love is subject to our changing circumstances.

**Godly Love is subject to our constant call
to follow Jesus.**

Human Love is a natural sensation of life in ourselves.

Godly Love is a supernatural act of life in Christ.

Human Love is expressed through action.

Godly Love is the action itself.

Being a Christian is all about Godly Love, but suppose someone comes up to you today and asks, "Are you a Christian?" What will you say? Will you think about a prayer you once uttered, rituals you participated in, or questions you answered? Will you think of your relationship with God or perhaps a promise to obey Him? Will you speak quickly and confidently, or take a moment to think about your answer and its implications? Will you think at all?

And suppose, if you say, "Yes," that person looks at you and in all seriousness whispers, "Prove it."

A new command I give you: Love one another. As I have loved you, so you must love one another. <u>By this all men will know that you are my disciples</u>, if you love one another. (John 13:34-35)

Dear children, let us not love with words or tongue but <u>with actions and in truth</u>. This then is how we

*know that we belong to the truth, and how we set our
hearts at rest in his presence whenever our hearts
condemn us.* (1 John 3:18-19)

Every day, we all need to prove it. Today love someone
you like…and someone you don't.
Take care and be God's.

From our readers…

*— You know it has to be a big deal if I am <u>choosing</u> to get
on-line <u>all by myself</u> just to send you this reply to your Note
I received today!!!! I want you to know that this Note came
just in time! I have been so caught up in how exciting it will
be to spend Valentine's Day with my boyfriend, that I had
almost forgotten about spending it with my one and only
<u>true love</u> and Creator, my Lord! I also like the ending
thought, "PROVE IT!" That is always something that's on
my mind!...Happy Valentine's Day!!!*

Easter, A New Beginning...for Easter

May God bless you this day...with a new beginning!

For the message of the cross is foolishness to those who are perishing, but to us who are being saved it is the power of God. 1 Corinthians 1:18

What does Easter mean to you?

For most of the people in this world, it means absolutely nothing. It's just another day to get up in the morning, work through daily routines, and go to bed at night. Then there's the reaction in what are traditionally regarded as "Christian" nations, such as the United States. And what is the most important emphasis there? Perhaps a day off from work. The "Easter" bunny and an egg hunt. Or maybe shopping throughout a weekend filled with special sales at bargain prices. More thought is given to what will be worn on Easter than what Easter is really about.

But the real tragedy lies within the Body of Christ itself, that community of people who call themselves Christians. We find the evidence of the problem in our churches where, regardless of size or grandeur, something truly sad occurs each Easter. A few years ago, a newspaper summed it up quite well:

Pews will be packed today as most of the world's Christians celebrate the basis of their faith — the resurrection of Jesus. Some worshippers are new to the faith and sing out with the enthusiasm of new discovery. Some are occasional Christians who come only out of a sense of habit or obligation. Others are beginning a spiritual search that will lead to a new commitment to their faith. And some, who grew up singing Easter hymns, won't be there at all. (Originally from **The Atlanta Journal,** Easter Day, April 16, 1995, and quoted in *Take The Stand* by Charles B. Graham)

Easter is not a show or a production. It's a time of serious reflection on who God is, who we are before Him, and what Jesus did on that cross. Every year I close my office on Good Friday so that I can spend time with my family and think about these things. Once we hiked deep into the woods, following a beautiful cascading brook through hemlocks, pines, firs and rhododendrons. After almost 4 miles of climbs and descents, the trail came to the top of a waterfall. We stayed there for a moment and then descended to a large open area at the bottom. Only then could we really see the true beauty of the falls. The water roared down across the rocks, cascading and freefalling to one level before dropping to the next, ending in a large peaceful pool. Tall evergreens stood on either side, drawing our attention toward the falls in the center and upward to the bright blue sky.

As I stood there, I thought how this waterfall would have looked much the same to Jesus 2000 years ago. Then it occurred to me. I wasn't able to appreciate the falls until I had gotten below them and could look upward. At the top, the water may have been moving a little faster but there was nothing special about it. My attention was drawn instead to the surrounding mountains, trees and scenery below. But at the bottom, the falls consumed me. There was nothing but the falls, and they were all I wanted to look at.

In the same way, we can't truly appreciate what Easter means until we get <u>below</u> the cross. We tend to think of the crucifixion on a more academic level, reading about the event as though it were a newspaper article. We see the three crosses at "eye level" and look down on the Roman Centurion as he reacts to the thunder and lightning. We see below us the women who cared for Jesus. Not too far away is Mary, His mother, being comforted by John. Everything unfolds as though we're watching a television show.

But when we take our rightful position...at the foot of the cross...everything changes. The thieves stand on either side like giant pines flanking THE cross, the object of our gaze which draws and holds our attention. Unaware of those around us, everything else fades as we stand motionless, taking in the awesomeness of the scene. Instead of watching <u>with</u> Jesus as He looks down on those gathered around Him, we now look UP into His eyes as He looks down on us! The crucifixion has become personal.

> *Let us fix our eyes on Jesus, the author and perfecter of our faith, who for the joy set before him endured the cross, scorning its shame, and sat down at the right hand of the throne of God.* Hebrews 12:2

What does Easter mean to you? My prayer is that Easter will mark for you a new beginning. A time in which you will find a new discovery in what Jesus did in His death and resurrection. A time of new enthusiasm for a spiritual search that will lead you in a new commitment to follow Him. A time when you can look up into His eyes and see nothing but the love God has for you...personally.

Take care and be God's.

From our readers...

— *Really deep and I liked it a lot. I tried the "look UP into His eyes as He looks down on us" from the cross. The difference was amazing.*

— *Awesome! It reminds me of a time that my husband was sharing about Easter with one of his employees and they truly did not have a clue what it was and why we get off work for Good Friday. It really opened my eyes!*

Christian Motherhood...for Mother's Day

May God bless you this day...and those we may have forgotten!

Please understand...I am not against mothers or that great day every year on which the stockholders of Hallmark rejoice in celebration...Mother's Day. However, I would like to share just a few observations, especially since we often fall into such a commercial routine, put a religious spin on it, and then wander away thinking we've done this great and uplifting thing...without ever realizing the pain we may have caused. Curious? Then read on.

Mother's Day is a day set aside for honoring mothers and motherhood. It is not observed throughout the world, contrary to the wishes of florists internationally, and is essentially an American thing, though it has been picked up by a few other countries. Would Jesus have supported a day set aside for honoring mothers? If we are talking about a female birth parent, I don't think so. (Please do not egg my house.) After all, consider teenage pregnancies and unmarried women choosing to have a child. For many, becoming a "mother" is not that difficult nor taken that seriously.

But what about "motherhood"? Now that's something entirely different. Searching through a dictionary, I arrived at the following definition of "motherhood": *the quality or state of a woman holding an authoritative or responsible position characterized by actions of love, guidance, nourishment, and watching over another.* I think Jesus would go for that, especially because it is not arbitrarily exclusive. If a woman chooses to live and act in that manner, she takes on this quality of motherhood.

In our society, we instead focus on a natural occurrence, that of childbirth. We may hear what a "good" mother should be, but when it comes down to it, you must have experienced childbirth or you can't get in the club. How many times even in church do we ask all mothers to stand, applaud their status, perhaps give them a gift, and tell them they are special...all because they were able to give birth to a child. And while caught up in this well-meaning display, we forget many others...those who are married and can't have children, those who have never married, those whose children have died, and those who have chosen not to have children. Sometimes we even exclude those who become mothers by adoption, as though that is somehow not worthy of recognition. And we do this without a thought of the consequences, even though such actions cause hurt, sadness, and despair. I know this is true. I watch the faces as they look down or away. I see the light leave their eyes as they struggle through the "celebration". And I see the vacant seats of those who just can't take it emotionally and so do not even come to God's house on Mother's Day.

Jesus would never have excluded anyone. He cared about the heart, not a status. He would have rejoiced in Christian Motherhood...not whether a woman was a natural mother. How do we know this? Once when He was told his family had come to see Him, Jesus pointed to His followers and said, *"Here are my mother and my brothers. For whoever does the will of my Father in heaven is my brother and sister and mother."* (Matthew 12:49-50)

With Jesus as our guide, Christian Motherhood then becomes:

The quality or state of a woman who, through obedience to the will of God, has chosen a position of responsibility in which she carries the authority of God's Word and puts it into practice by loving, guiding, nourishing, and watching over others.

A member of this Motherhood may sing in the choir or

teach young children. She may serve the youth or help the seniors. She may be married or single, have a child or have none. But regardless of her status in life, she should never be excluded...never made less worthy than others...and never, ever be left feeling so helplessly alone.

A few months ago I attended the funeral of my wife's Great Aunt Ruth. She was one of eleven children, and probably from trying just to be noticed, she had become quite a funny, delightful character. She married young in rural Georgia at a time when large families were a source of great pride. But in all her many years of married life, she was never able to have a child. Whenever I was around her, I would watch the way she so easily took to children and see the immense joy she had in just being with them. I always felt sad that she never had any of her own.

Her funeral was held at a little country church and it was there that I really got to understand what Christian Motherhood was all about. In addition to the relatives who arrived, there was an even larger family that came. Men and women of all ages, teenagers and children. After the service I heard one man in his fifties say, "Yeah, Miss Ruth taught me Sunday School." "Really?" a teenager replied. "Me, too!" Women in their forties shared stories about Miss Ruth while those younger and older waited to tell theirs.

And it all became clear. Ruth never had children the old fashioned way. But she did have children...oh, she definitely had children...and grandchildren and great-grandchildren. She was obedient to God, shared His Word with all of those people, and cared for them. And they loved her.

As you think about Mother's Day, remember your mother, but don't forget all of these other wonderful Godly women. They are every bit a part of the Christian Motherhood. And when you get a chance, say a prayer for them. For many, it is still a difficult thing not having children or not having them anymore, and on top of it all, they have to put up with the rest of us who sometimes forget.

To everyone in the Christian Motherhood, we love you! Take care and be God's.

From our readers...

— *As a 32 year old, baby-less woman, I have felt some of what you expressed. Through spiritual mentoring, God is allowing me to use my design as a woman to nurture, encourage and teach younger women. As I mature, I can sense and have even heard the thoughts, "...aren't you going to get married...your clock is ticking?" In God's sovereignty, I know God doesn't have clocks. There are no tick tocks in eternity. God is timeless. I'm so grateful that my heart has been settled long ago to trust God in this detail of my life. For now, I enjoy watching the younger ones learn to eat solid foods, walk, and soar on the wings of eagles in their spiritual lives.*

— *Your Note was truly a note of encouragement for me and I read it with tears in my eyes. My beloved husband of 33 years and I have never been able to have children. It's been the only real disappointment in our marriage. We grieved for many years but then came to see it as the Lord's will as we threw ourselves into youth work even before we married. We've been blessed to have "kids" all over the world, many of whom are now in the ministry...Even though many of these kids think of us in a parental context, none of them remember us in that way on Mother's Day or Father's Day. Since my own Mother has been promoted to Heaven, I don't even go to church on Mother's Day. It hurts too badly. Thank you for your very sensitive insight. I wish more people, especially our pastors, thought that way.*

— *Thank you for including me in this. I was actually feeling very down on Sunday. And yes, at church they had all the mothers stand and gave them all a rose. I somehow felt that I wasn't included in that because I've not given birth. Usually it doesn't bother me, but every Mother's Day I feel like I've missed the boat...I'm going to print this and read it every year as a reminder.*

— Your Note on Aunt Ruth reminded me of two of mine who couldn't have children but reared most of our small community, taught all of us in Sunday School, and then advised our youth groups. One died at 94...her funeral was full of people of all ages telling their stories of how she had been the factor in her life that made them make the positive choices she had made. The second had cancer last year...they believe she is cancer free now...but the outpouring of people who came to support and cheer her on was unlike any I have ever seen for a cancer patient (who are typically avoided like the plague). I have always sent her a mother's day card...and she ALWAYS cries.

A Time to Remember...for Memorial Day

May God bless you this day...and those who sacrifice!

...a time to love and a time to hate, a time for war and a time for peace. Ecclesiastes 3:8

May God arise, may his enemies be scattered; may his foes flee before him. Psalms 68:1

Memorial Day weekend was a little different one year. Instead of picnics or family gatherings, I helped my mother move...loading boxes, throwing away junk, and just being glad I didn't have to move the furniture. I found lots of "relics", many of which I have no idea why they still exist. My biology test from junior high? I mean, really. And as I sifted and separated the "keeps" from the "throw-aways", I sometimes thought of how other families were enjoying the weekend...cookouts and barbecues, eating watermelon or making ice cream...maybe even seeing a parade or taking in a ball game. And I missed it.

So I sat on the basement floor, looking through boxes of old stuff. There was the baseball cap I had worn when I was 10, a school paper bearing the forged signature of my mother (I still have no idea how that got there), and even a few notes from my wife when we were in high school. Normal memorabilia. But hidden in all of this, I also found treasure: an old newspaper, a worn letter, and a metal bracelet.

The newspaper – *The Fort Jackson Journal*'s Memorial Day weekend issue for 1954. Inside is a story of the 516th Airborne Infantry and its campaigns of Lorraine, St. Mihiel and Meuese-Argonne during World War I and the Battle of Bastogne in World War II. There's an announcement for the upcoming "10th" anniversary of D-Day. An article somberly tells of plans to bury unidentified U.S. servicemen killed in

Korea, a "conflict" which had ended the year before. And there, on page 3, looking like a kid out of high school, is my dad, Cpl. Charles Graham of the 101st Airborne.

I remember…that he first entered the Army while the Korean Conflict was still going on. His unit was eventually sent there to join in the fight, but he and one other were ordered to stay at Fort Jackson. Most of his unit never returned. As I looked at the man in the picture, it was hard to imagine he was ever so young or what he must have thought of that war so far away. Many of his friends died. He would remember them, but as for those years…well, it seemed to be his greatest desire to forget that time.

The letter – still inside its envelope, also bearing the designation of the 101st Airborne, but from a different era. The letter, dated "Thursday Night, Feb. 26, '70", had come from what was then called South Vietnam and was written by my dad's younger brother. In it he told us about the R&R he had in Hawaii with his young wife; of his faithful army dog, Rinny; and how much he looked forward to coming home. And in July of 1970, he did come home, all safe and sound…and we were very grateful.

I remember…the nightly news showing combat in the jungles, bombs being dropped from jets streaking across the Asian sky, and the daily revised counts of the dead and missing in action. Everywhere there was the Vietnam War and its influence. It was a time of anger and confusion…of patriotism and heroism as well as civil unrest and demonstrations. And a time when young men and women left a land where they risked their lives every day to come home where many were treated as objects of shame and disgust.

The bracelet – a single piece of shiny metal with black letters across the top. On February 17, 1972, Major Robert H. Irwin, pilot, and Capt. Edwin A. Hawley, Jr., weapons and systems operator, were flying their Phantom F4D over North Vietnam when, about 15 miles west of the city of Vinh in the

Quang Binh Province, their aircraft was shot down.

I remember...a POW/MIA program that distributed bracelets with the names of missing servicemen. The one I received in the spring of 1972 bore the name "Capt. Edwin Hawley". I wore it and prayed for him day after day. Then on February 14, 1973, a number of POWs were released by the North Vietnamese. Some time later, I watched a news report about some of them. One by one, most very thin and weak, they exited the planes that had brought them home. The camera focused on one young man, still showing signs of injuries sustained when he had ejected. His name appeared across the bottom of the TV...Capt. Edwin Hawley.

It's odd how things work out. That weekend I thought I was missing a holiday, but I almost missed what the weekend is all about...remembering. By remembering the reality of the horror of war, the death of family and friends, the sacrifice of those in the service...maybe we won't forget to honor those who have protected us in years past or who protect us now. We enjoy freedoms the rest of the world can only dream about because these people have sacrificed their own freedom. And we live a blessed life in this country because God has given us His blessing. I hope we will never forget the sacrifice or the blessing.

Remember those who have died and take every opportunity to thank those who have served and continue to serve. Such recognition should never be confined to just one weekend.

On my list, to Roy Graham (Navy, World War II), Charles Graham (Army, Korean Conflict), Dale Smith (Navy, Korean Conflict), Eddie Graham (Vietnam War), David Graham (The Gulf War)...we love you all. And to Jim Freeman and the ministry of Task Force Patriot, thanks for helping us remember.

Take care and be God's.

From our readers...

— *God bless you...for remembering in the true spirit.*

— *Thanks for remembering what yesterday was all about...*

— *War is an ever-present challenge here in Mindanao. We are always at war! Not only physical wars, but also spiritual wars. We do know, however, who is the victor! PTL!*

I especially enjoyed your Note about going through your "junk", but in reality real treasures! It's always good to reflect on the sacrifices of others for what we enjoy today. Can't help but think of the sacrifices of US military people here in the Philippines too! My husband, who is Filipino, once asked me this question: "What makes the USA such a prosperous and blessed nation?" I thought about a lot of answers, but his remark to me was this: "I believe it's because the USA has given of their resources financially, opened their borders to developing nations, and for sacrificing their military personnel on foreign fields." I can't help but agree! If we ever stop doing these "things" for other countries, God will remove the blessings!

A Plainer Walk *by Beverly Graham...*
for Father's Day

May God bless you this day...as others observe your walk with Him!

Father's Day in the U.S. is a day celebrated by Hallmark Cards & Gift Shops, men's clothiers, hardware stores, and sporting good suppliers across the country. As a part of my present one year, my lovely wife wrote a *Note of Encouragement*. She takes this idea of "Father's" Day and goes to a deeper level that affects all of us, regardless of whether we are fathers or even parents, for that matter. Read carefully, and apply these words to your own life.

Take care and be God's.

"A Plainer Walk"

If you have read a few *Notes of Encouragement*, I'm sure you have been able to determine how much my husband enjoys hiking. Over the years our family has spent countless hours walking on trails through the woods, on paths through seashore parks, down the beach, around the neighborhood ... you get the picture. Walking and talking. Sharing our dreams and disappointments. Reflecting on the wonder of God's creations. As the family photographer, I have taken many pictures of my husband leading and our three children following, falling in line behind him while walking down a trail. So, when I saw a calligraphy version of the poem below, I had to have it. It has hung in our home for many years as a constant reminder of the impact we have on our children and the responsibilities we have as parents.

"Walk A Little Plainer, Daddy"

"Walk a little plainer, Daddy," said the little boy so frail.
"I'm following in your footsteps and I don't want to fail.
Sometimes your steps are very plain,
sometimes they are hard to see.
So walk a little plainer Daddy, for you are leading me."
"I know that once you walked this way so many years ago
And what you did along the way I'd really like to know.
For sometimes when I'm tempted, I don't know what to do.
So walk a little plainer Daddy for I must follow you."
"Someday when I'm grown up, you are like I want to be.
Then I will have a little boy who will want to follow me.
And I would want to lead him right,
and help him to be true.
So walk a little plainer, Daddy, for we must follow you."
(author unknown)

As Christians, however, our roles become even more pronounced. Not only are we the role models for our children, but we also become mentors for our brothers and sisters in Christ. While as Christians our goal is to become more Christ-like and our ultimate mentor is Christ Himself, we all choose "leaders" to follow along the road of life. In fact, someone may have chosen us as their model without sharing their choice with us. So we all need to "walk a little plainer" so that people can see Christ glorified through us.

In all things showing yourself to be a pattern of good works; in doctrine showing integrity, reverence, incorruptibility, sound speech that cannot be condemned, that one who is an opponent may be ashamed, having nothing evil to say of you. (Titus 2:7-8 NKJV)

From our readers...

— *We are sometimes the only example of Jesus people will see.*

— *I never see the framed copy of "Walk a Little Plainer" that I don't stop to read it again. What a beautiful Note...thank you for a job well done.*

Our Legacy...What Will They Remember?
...for July 4

May God bless you this day...with a legacy to give!

July the Fourth in the U.S. is known as Independence Day. It is the day Americans come together to celebrate. Just exactly what it is they're celebrating is different with each person. For some it's a day off from work or bargain sales at the mall. For others, it's picnics in the park and fireworks at night. For many, it's the time when we come to honor that most glorious of food...that divine manna from heaven... barbecue. But even as good as barbecue is, that's not really what this day is supposed to be about.

This day is about legacy, that which has been handed down from our ancestors. Something for us to remember, cherish, and protect so that we can then pass it on to a new generation. It's about honored rights and amazing accomplishments. It's the history of this great nation — what we can hold dear that was right and what we can learn from that was wrong. And it is a time of reflection, a time to remember the sacrifices that have been made. Hardships, tragedies and the many lost lives given for a noble purpose. Sacrifices of which we are the beneficiaries.

Each year as this holiday approaches, I start to think of what all this "remembering" is about. What's the point? Is it simply to glorify our past, this nation, or ourselves? To show the world just how wonderful we think we are? To sing patriotic songs and light a firecracker?

I believe the point of remembering is this: to use the lessons of yesterday in what we do today as we work for a better tomorrow. Whatever the plan or goal, we look to legacies, those things which are handed down from the past. In remembering, we look to the legacy of freedom that was fought for and left for us to enjoy. Freedom from tyranny.

Freedom to pursue happiness. Freedom to govern ourselves. Freedom to worship God. But sometimes I wonder if in this country, we truly honor and cherish such freedoms. Do we understand what an incredible gift from God these freedoms are? Do we realize a war is raging to destroy them?

In the Christian world today, there are many battles. Some are fought in faraway lands, such as The Philippines, Togo, Venezuela, and Zimbabwe. Others are closer to home, like New York, Houston, Miami, and Atlanta. Wherever God's people seek to spread the Gospel, there are those who fight to stop it. But there is another battle going on. It is much more subtle, much more deadly, and much more costly. That battle directly affects all others. Though often more obvious in groups and organizations, it is actually waged on a purely individual scale. It is the battle for our integrity.

As Christians we are called by God to hold firm to a certain code, a specific standard of conduct. As John wrote:

We know that we have come to know Him if we obey his commands. The man who says, "I know him," but does not do what he commands is a liar, and the truth is not in him. But if anyone obeys his word, God's love is truly made complete in him. This is how we know we are in him: Whoever claims to live in him must walk as Jesus did.
1 John 2:3-6

What is that code or standard? It is the Word of God! We obey God's commands. We pattern our lives after Jesus. We love each other. We encourage and build each other up. We do good so that even those who don't know Him will praise our Heavenly Father. We don't merely talk about being followers of Christ, we act like...become...no, we are followers of Christ. And when the battles come, we stand in His strength. We do not take the trash this world has to offer. We take a stand. We hold firm. We have integrity. And only through such integrity is there real freedom!

Now the Lord is the Spirit, and where the Spirit of the Lord is, there is freedom. 2 Corinthians 3:17-18

Recently I've seen…a Christian corporation underpay its employees, telling them it's for their own good…another break commitments because it wasn't making enough profit…a Christian church allow the worship of a pagan god in its sanctuary…a Christian denomination proudly publish the book of a senator who believes that abortion is not a proper subject for the law…a ministry embrace false teachings on prayer as a means of gaining more supporters, more exposure, and more money.

What is the legacy we can leave to the next generation of Christians? Will it be financial holdings or annual revenues? Will it be the size of a church, the number of books sold, or the global presence of a ministry? Will it be measured in terms of the world's standards…or by God's?

What you do today will be the legacy for Christians tomorrow as they seek to do God's will in the future. Do you have integrity? Do you know freedom? Do you have independence from the demands and pressures of this world? Do you obey God and walk as Jesus did, no matter the cost? Will your legacy mean anything at all? It's your choice. What will you leave people to remember?

Take care and be God's.

From our readers…

— *Thanks Chuck for your thoughts and comments . We heard President Bush give his speech in Normandy, France last night on TV. It was very inspiring and well said.*

Looking at all those 9,000 plus graves was a reminder of the great prices paid for freedom. We all have much to thank God in regards to lives given on our behalf. Blessings as we all seek to leave a Godly legacy to the next generations!

Hope Lives On *by Beverly Graham*
...for September 11

May God bless you this day...with hope that lives on!

On the morning of September 11, 2001, the unbelievable took place. Planes filled with innocent passengers and crew became weapons of war, crashing into the towers of the World Trade Center. Then news spread of a third plane striking the Pentagon. A fourth fell short of its target due to the heroic efforts of a few who would not allow terrorists to accomplish their deadly mission. Many were dead; many more injured.

Tragedy always brings deep loss and grief. Even when surrounded by many, we can be overwhelmed by loneliness, as though God has turned His back on us, ignoring our pain. So we ask...no we demand to know... "My God, how could you allow this to happen!?!" Yet we already know the answer. Evil exists in this world. It is real. It has lived among us because <u>mankind</u> allowed it into God's creation. And ever since, this world has not been safe.

But there is hope. Though we are but strangers in this world, we are never alone for God is always with us. (Matthew 28:20) When tragedy comes, God hurts deeply and cries with us. (John 11:33-36) He knows what it's like to feel alone, for even He cried out, "My God, my God, why have you forsaken me?" (Matthew 27:46) And yet we have not been abandoned! Jesus was sending us a message of hope and assurance, not of desperation, when He uttered those words beginning Psalms 22...a passage that reaches this remarkable conclusion:

I will declare your name to my brothers; in the congregation I will praise you. You who fear the LORD, praise him! All you descendants of Jacob,

honor him! Revere him, all you descendants of Israel! <u>For he has not despised or disdained the suffering of the afflicted one; he has not hidden his face from him but has listened to his cry for help</u>.
Psalms 22:22-24

Even when tragedy strikes and we are filled with sorrow…hope lives on!

Take care and be God's.

"Hope Lives On"

Hope lives on. In the midst of the great tragedy that struck America on September 11, *hope* lives on. As the world watched in horror the aftermath of the terrorist attack on the United States, *hope* lives on. The media coverage of these events brought to us stories of countless families whose lives were forever changed by these events. And yet…*hope* lives on.

Like many other Americans at that time, I longed for a way to help, a way to reach out to all those who were waiting to hear news of their loved ones who were at the World Trade Center. My opportunity came through my employer, BellSouth, who was asked to assist the Federal Emergency Management Agency by setting up a call center to record cell phone and pager numbers of missing people from their friends and family members who would share that information. These numbers would then be used to send out a signal and use a technology similar to GPS (global positioning system) in an attempt to locate the devices and hopefully their owners.

As I listened to the callers, I was struck by their composure and the gratitude they expressed. And yet I noticed they had something else in common. Each of them was looking for some small thread of *hope* … *hope* for news of a miracle, *hope* that their loved one would be found alive. At the end of my shifts, I thought about the conversations I'd had. A fireman's wife who knew her husband's station would have been first on the scene. A wife of a businessman who was attending a meeting at the WTC. A sister who kept calling her brother's cell phone just so she could hear his voice. A friend of an invalid woman whose daughter worked at the WTC. A woman who had talked until early that Tuesday morning with her friend. A coworker who received a page from his boss checking to see if he was okay, but who wasn't heard from again. These are only a few of the people I spoke with during the long hours I answered calls. And for every one of them, I longed to give them the *hope* they were searching for.

The next week, on Saturday, September 22, I had another opportunity. I met with a group of believers on top of Stone Mountain, just outside of Atlanta, Georgia USA. For three hours, we talked...we shared...we prayed. During this time, one of the youth with us reminded me just how to give others the *hope* they longed for. As we stayed within our close fellowship, she spent much of her time reaching out to strangers on the Mountain, sharing her faith in Jesus Christ...the only true *Hope* for mankind. The *Hope* that never lets us down. The Hope that is always with us.

And so *Hope* lives on. Will you share the true *Hope* with someone today?

May the God of hope fill you with all joy and peace as you trust in Him, so that you may overflow with hope by the power of the Holy Spirit. Romans 15:13

From our readers...

— *Please pass on my appreciation to Beverly for her Note!
I work for Sprint, and we've heard stories also, of the positive impacts that telecommunications made during the
whole tragedy.*

— *Best Note of Encouragement yet.*

The Heart of Thanksgiving...for Thanksgiving

May God bless you this day...as you give thanks.

Each year as another Thanksgiving rolls around, I find myself preparing for this special day. Not by going to those "once in a lifetime sales" or planning for the next family gathering. The spirit within me leads me to consider what Thanksgiving means and the blessings I've received over the past year. And as I think of family, friends, happy times, and the work of this wonderful ministry God has allowed me to be a part of, I feel drawn, compelled really, to remember a Thanksgiving not so very long ago. And everything once again falls back into His perspective.

Thanksgiving Day: A national holiday set apart for giving thanks to God, celebrated on the fourth Thursday of November in the U.S. and on the second Monday of October in Canada.

"A national holiday"...a day for the entire country to have a special observation and celebration...

***News Bulletin — September 11...two planes strike the towers of the World Trade Center which collapse, killing hundreds and injuring thousands... a third plane strikes the Pentagon...a fourth crashes in Pennsylvania... the nation goes into a state of alert as President Bush rallies Americans and U.S. allies to unite against terrorism...churches fill for prayer with people who usually don't attend.

"set apart for"...separated from all others for the especially significant purpose of...

***News Bulletin — Two American foreign aid workers are tried in Afghanistan for sharing the Gospel of Jesus Christ, a crime punishable by death…allies attack Afghanistan's ruling Taliban and go after Osama bin Laden…church attendance drops slightly though leaders continue to call for prayer.

"giving"…offering, providing, speaking, and showing…

***News Bulletin** — Anthrax kills…the bombing and destruction of Afghanistan continues…the world learns of life there, one filled with orphans, infant mortality, horrible treatment of women, fear, land mines, and death…church attendance continues to drop.

"thanks"…a personal acknowledgment of a gift or benefit, expressing gratitude and appreciation…

***News Bulletin** — Stock markets suffer…corporations cut back…layoffs…men and women see their "faith" shaken as they lose jobs and financial security…many question what they have to give thanks for and why God hasn't done anything…others question God's existence as they see a world of fear and evil.

"to God"…that perfect, all-powerful, all-knowing being, who

- prepared a beautiful place for His first human creatures, who betrayed Him,

- watched in sadness as mankind doomed this world to sin, evil, death and destruction,

- became a man to teach the truth and die as the only possible sacrifice for mankind's sins,

- gave mankind the opportunity to live with Him now and forever, and

- is with us as we journey through the pain of this world into the paradise of the next...

Thanksgiving Day finds many who are in grief and mourning for the loss of a loved one, lost marriages, lost children, lost friendships...lost futures, hopes and dreams. There is loneliness, bitterness, and despair. They question God, "Why haven't You done something? Why didn't You stop it? Why have I lost so much?" And giving thanks is difficult.

But there is a gift greater than anything we obtain in this world...our relationship with God. Jesus did not come to give us a great life here. He came to give us eternal life, a life that will continue into peace and joy when the tragedies, pain, sorrow, evil, hatred, and death of this world forever end. And even when horrible things go on around us, we can still look to Thanksgiving as...

that special day, separated from all other days for the significant purpose of offering and showing our personal expressions of gratitude to God for that priceless gift...His love which allows us forever to call Him Father and Friend and assures us that He will never leave us.

Enter his gates with thanksgiving and his courts with praise; give thanks to him and praise his name. For the LORD is good and his love endures forever; his faithfulness continues through all generations. Psalms 100:4-5

Thanks, Father.
Take care and be God's.

From our readers...

— *"Thank you for giving to the Lord – I am a life that was changed."*

Living Christmas Throughout the Year
...for Christmas

May God bless you this day...with a new day!

Therefore, if anyone is in Christ, he is a new creation; the old has gone, the new has come!
2 Corinthians 5:17

This time of year we are often caught in a tremendous whirlwind. We feverishly make detailed plans, hurry through Thanksgiving, and rush into a Yuletide season of shopping and buying, hopelessly spinning out of control until we find ourselves Christmas night sitting on the floor and wondering what happened to all our plans. Then with just enough time to catch our breath, we see the world start spinning again as we run into the next week, New Year's Day, and the promise of resolutions we'll probably never keep. We remember to honor our "traditions" while forgetting the reason for the season.

In all of English literature, there is one character I have studied many times. I guess what I have most enjoyed about him was his attitude toward Christmas and what it really means. He did not get swept away with commercialism or the need to give a gift simply for the sake of giving a gift. He never bowed down to traditions, but saw through them to what they actually stood for and what was important. He shunned false displays of kindness, and became a true example of charity.

And what exactly did he do? He fed the hungry. He aided the sick. He assisted the poor. He provided for the homeless and those in prison. He embraced the wealthy and beggars alike. He offered everyone he met a ready smile, genuine kindness, and sincere respect. And he went to church and worshiped the true reason for this season. But most important, he did not limit his actions or attitudes to this one day, but sustained them throughout the year. There was never a better friend, employer or person in his city. His example so affected others that it was <u>always</u> said of him that he knew the right way to honor Christmas. And this man's name was... Ebenezer Scrooge.

Surprised? Isn't it interesting how we tend to dwell on someone's past and not focus on the person they've become or can become? Ebenezer Scrooge was a horrible, hated creature, who looked upon Christmas as "a poor excuse for picking a man's pocket every twenty-fifth of December". Yet he became a kind, loving man who saw in Christmas Day the call to honor God and love others...every day!

January 1 may mark the beginning of a new year, but let's commit to see every day as a new day, one devoted to knowing God better, following Him more closely, and sharing with others the incredible joy we have been given. Let us also commit to encourage those men and women who have dedicated their lives to our Lord's service. Remember them in your prayers and encourage them often.

Therefore we do not lose heart. Though outwardly we are wasting away, yet inwardly we are being renewed day by day. 2 Corinthians 4:16

And I hope you will join with us in praying for and thanking those Christian brothers and sisters, clergy and laity alike, who have encouraged us in **Ciloa** as we have tried to encourage others. They carry the true meaning of Christmas with them. "May that be truly said of us, and all of us! And so, as Tiny Tim observed, God bless Us, Every One!"

Take care and be God's.

From our readers...

— *...my name cried out at me from your* Note *and said,
"What am I doing?" And I cry out to you and say, "Surely
you know...." For you see, I perhaps possess more of
Scrooge's former traits than I do his later traits. But I will
say this, I know what Christmas stands for in my book and
while it is not about buying gifts, it* does *have something to
do with giving.*

A Note of Thanks

Acts of Encouragers

May God work through you this day...to touch others.

A fifth grade class goes to a college where they see students demonstrating in response to U.S. military operations in a foreign country. The students are making posters, individual expressions of peace to hang in the student center. When the fifth graders ask if they can help, a student leader welcomes them to the cause. Eager to express their own individual ideas of peace, the fifth graders shock the college students with posters that declare, "God's got the whole world in His hands" and "Jesus is the Prince of Peace".

A high school football coach works in a public school system filled with countless do's and don'ts about what teachers can say to students. He really cares for the future of his team. In spite of the risk to his job, he shares his faith in Jesus Christ with his players and strives to be an example to them.

A rheumatologist leaves a lucrative practice at least once each year, but not to take a vacation. He goes to Central America, as he's done for a long time, to be a source of Christian help to the people there — whether that's in providing medical attention or helping build a bridge.

A manager works with a telecommunications company. She's divorced and her kids are grown. In spite of having no previous training, she takes a leave from work, goes through extensive studies, and becomes a part-time missionary working in medical relief efforts...in the Ukraine, Philippines and Iraq.

An expert in international insurance builds a highly successful business, respected throughout the field. With associates thinking he's crazy, he leaves the security of his practice and income to become...a youth minister. He makes very little but he gets to help mold the next generation of Christian leaders.

A vice president of a large corporation is chosen to manage the company's United Way effort. When employees complain of that organization's funding of abortion efforts, he shares his own views as a Christian. The company, "embarrassed" by such expressions, summarily removes him as a corporate officer. He loses his position with the company, but not his relationship with God.

These stories are true. They're about real life, ordinary people...just like you and me...who chose to do something sadly unique in this world. They chose to follow God and not act like they'd never met Him. They chose to BE a Christian in their lives, and not just for a few hours on Sunday.

The man who says, 'I know [Jesus],' but does not do what he commands is a liar, and the truth is not in him. But if anyone obeys his word, God's love is truly made complete in him. This is how we know we are in him: Whoever claims to live in him must walk as Jesus did. (1 John 2:4-6)

Do you walk as Jesus did? Is it important to you or just something for whenever you have the time? Is your life the truth or a lie? Remember what's important...it isn't the work you personally do that eternally affects others, but the work God can do through you. Do you give Him the opportunity?

Several years ago a young boy dreamed of playing on his school's baseball team. But he got cancer. Still, he did what he could and helped out the team as a student manager. The cancer would go into remission, but always return. Yet through it all, he had a peace that only God can give. Many people prayed for this boy as he fought the disease. They talked to him, visited with him, came to love him, and through him, they experienced God. Eventually the cancer grew worse and the boy could no longer be with his team. When he died, the sign at his church said simply, "Safe at home". But God was not finished with this life.

A memorial service was held on his school's baseball field and thousands of students attended. There they heard the Gospel shared by Brett Butler, a former major league baseball player who had befriended the boy. Students, athletes and non-athletes alike, came to Christ that day and later as well in churches throughout the area. Students from surrounding schools heard of this boy's love for God and were deeply moved. They shared his story with their families and friends, a story that even found its way into the largest newspaper in the southeastern U.S. He could never have foreseen that his life and the God-given love in him would touch so many people. He just wanted to please his Lord.

Encouraging others means using the opportunities that God brings. We may not know the reach of our actions, but He does. The only thing He asks is that we truly and sincerely love one another. Thank you for allowing us the opportunity to share a part of our lives and encourage you along the Way in yours. And to all those who have lifted *Ciloa* up in your prayers, sent us responses to the *Notes*, and shared your hopes for this ministry...thanks for the encouragement!

Take care and be God's.

Chuck

Topic Index

Page numbers reference the beginning page
for the *Note* containing that topic.

X

Y

Z

Scripture Index

Page numbers reference the beginning page
for the *Note* containing that scripture.

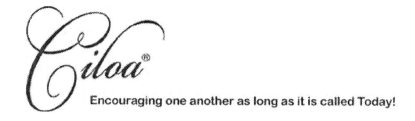

Encouraging one another as long as it is called Today!

Ciloa
Christ Is Lord Of All

About Ciloa

Ciloa is a Christ-centered organization devoted to the Biblical principals of "encouraging one another". Founded in 1997, *Ciloa* works with ministries, churches, businesses and other organizations challenging the hearts and minds of God's people to demonstrate their love for others, and in so doing, show the world that we follow Jesus Christ.

Ciloa encourages individuals around the world through *"__A Note of Encouragement__"* each week to seek God and to encourage one another.

Ciloa also provides training in Christian encouragement and edification through *"__The Encourager's Walk__"*, a Biblically-based instructional series of seminars which explores the importance of Encouragement in the Body of Christ, its many different forms, and the Christian's role in encouraging others.

Ciloa is a 501(c)(3) non-profit organization.

But encourage one another daily, as long as it is called Today, so that none of you may be hardened by sin's deceitfulness. Hebrews 3:13

About the Author

Charles B. Graham is Founder and Executive Director of *Ciloa,* a Christ-centered organization devoted to the Biblical principals of "encouraging one another". He is an accomplished author, speaker, attorney and Christian counselor.

Mr. Graham's previous book, ***Take The Stand,*** challenges Christians to carefully consider what it means to follow Jesus and how their Christian witness affects those around them. Mr. Graham speaks with groups and Christian organizations on encouragement, Christian principals, and reconciliation.

You may learn more about *Ciloa* and Mr. Graham, and also subscribe to "*A Note of Encouragement",* at our website.

www.Ciloa.org

Printed in the United States
23071LVS00002B/67-558